Robert M. La Follette
and the
Insurgent Spirit

David P. Thelen

Robert M. La Follette
and the
Insurgent Spirit

Edited by Oscar Handlin

The University of Wisconsin Press

Published 1985

The University of Wisconsin Press
114 North Murray Street
Madison, Wisconsin 53715

The University of Wisconsin Press, Ltd.
1 Gower Street
London WC1E 6HA, England

First Wisconsin printing
Originally published in 1976 by Little, Brown and Company (Inc.)

Printed in the United States of America

Cover photograph courtesy of
The State Historical Society of Wisconsin

Library of Congress Cataloging-in-Publication Data
Thelen, David P. (David Paul)
Robert M. La Follette and the insurgent spirit.
Bibliography: pp. 195–199.
Includes index.
1. La Follette, Robert M. (Robert Marion), 1855–1925.
2. Progressivism (United States politics)
3. United States — Politics and government — 1865–1933.
4. Legislators — United States — Biography.
5. United States. Congress — Biography.
E664.L16T52   1985   973.91'092'4 [B]   85-40844
ISBN 0-299-10644-6 (pbk.)

For
Jennifer and Jeremy
Two Budding Insurgents

Contents

Preface

A NEW EDITION of a book provides an opportunity to address a new generation of readers whose assumptions about the book's subject differ radically from those for whom the book was originally written. Although the chronological distance from the early 1970s, when I wrote this book, to 1985, when I write this introduction, is relatively short, it has been long enough to transform beyond recognition many prevailing assumptions about how people can and should control their lives.

For many readers in the 1970s, as for Robert La Follette in the early twentieth century, collective, public, and political action seemed a natural way for people to try to control their lives. Even the most personal interactions implied relationships of power and politics. Finding personal fulfillment in collective struggle to create a more just society, viewing government and politics as means to create that better world, readers of that period saw the history of earlier political reformers and radicals as their own history from which to derive inspiration and instruction.

I wrote this book in that spirit of inspiration and instruction. Robert M. La Follette *was* inspiring, perhaps the most popular and respected radical in modern American history. He had grappled with the fundamental problems of how to make government respond to the wishes of the majority in a world that large-scale industrial capitalism was rapidly transforming. But I also had a moral to extract. I believed that the failure of the progressive movement that carried La Follette to prominence held wider meanings for other movements of political reform and radicalism. At a time when it was fashionable to explore the economic system and related dominant cultural values to explain failure of earlier democratic movements, I wanted to direct the same spirit of probing criticism toward political structures and traditions. La Follette's limitations as a political spokesperson for democratic aspirations were fundamentally limitations of the political structures and traditions in which he operated, not personal limitations or limitations of the economic system. The first priority for the 1970s, I believed, was to refashion the political system so that it could better fulfill democratic dreams.

I fear that we now face a more formidable obstacle: many readers believe that they can best control their lives by improving their personalities and personal circumstances, and that the quest for control is fundamentally an individualistic search for self-fulfillment. The forms of collective control — politics and government —appear very remote, even irrelevant, to those with a faith in individual control. To such readers the story of Robert La Follette is even more important than to those of the early 1970s. It tells us that there have been times when people did turn to collective action and politics to control their lives. And they did it in many ways. If there were such times in the past, there will certainly be such times again. What will cause the change will be the rediscovery that people require the help of others to control their lives. At that point politics will once again seem close at hand.

Robert La Follette and the progressive movement remain for us as a case study of what people learned when they entered the political arena in order to organize their collective aspirations to control their lives. The basic fact about the progressive movement, as about most political movements, is that it changed over time as its members learned new things and encountered new problems. La Follette's career helps to illuminate those changes.

Progressivism began in the 1890s as a series of angry, unorganized, grassroots campaigns by consumers and taxpayers to challenge the legitimacy of privileged and concentrated wealth and power. This early phase of the movement I have called *insurgency.* As insurgent consumers and taxpayers moved from their local origins to demand changes at the state and national level, however,

they discovered problems they had never imagined, and their movement lost some of the radical power that had been part of its original grassroots impetus. By the early 1910s, accelerating greatly as
a result of the domestic consequences of World War I, progressivism became less an uprising by consumers and taxpayers and more
a movement by farmers and workers to seek relief in their work-
places. People tended to form self-conscious groups based on their
jobs as farmers, workers, and professionals, and to seek help from
government for their groups. Since that group identity accompanied
industrialization wherever it occurred, I have followed the convention of assigning the term *modernization* to this process. In so doing,
however, I do not mean to imply that the process was inevitable
and desirable or that Americans abandoned their traditional values
when industrialization transformed the surfaces of their lives. In any
case, it was insurgency, not modernization, that gave American progressivism its distinctive elements.

As a popular politician, La Follette was less interested in
academic terms than in winning popular support and votes. He
wanted to dethrone corporate control of government; thus, he shifted
his appeal from consumers and taxpayers to farmers and workers
as he saw how voters were changing their own expectations of how
to seek relief from corporate domination. His personal fame rested
less on ideologies than on his special kind of courage, a courage
that created his nickname, Fighting Bob. Once convinced that he
was speaking for majority opinion on a subject, he would defy mighty
leaders, powerful institutions, and ancient traditions until, as he
said in his favorite motto, "the will of the people shall be the law
of the land."

Many people have contributed to this book. Curtis Synhorst, Fred Rich, and William D. Rogers helped with its research,
and Synhorst and Rich gave its first draft a very perceptive reading.
Thomas B. Alexander and his assistants Harry Holmes and Ross
Cameron ran computer programs on the roll calls for La Follette's
twenty years in the Senate, and, although the results do not appear
here in quantitative form, they lie behind some of the generaliza-
tions about insurgent blocs in the Senate. Discussions with Wil-

liam Beach, Noble Cunningham, Dale Grinder, Edward Purcell, Arvarh Strickland, Selwyn Troen, and William Wieck helped to sharpen some of the issues. The University of Missouri–Columbia Research Council generously supported a summer in Washington, D.C. Richard S. Kirkendall, Michael J. Cassity, and the late John C. Rainbolt gave their encouragement and critical advice to me in all phases of developing the book. Although Oscar Handlin disagreed with my interpretation of La Follette and his significance, he made excellent editorial suggestions about how to cut a much longer manuscript. Peter Marshall offered many helpful suggestions about the manuscript. In addition to constant encouragement, stimulating company, and good critical advice, Robert Griffith gave the manuscript detailed suggestions for revision that helped to shape its final form. Marian Ferguson, Deborah Otaguro, and Kathleen Field of Little, Brown contributed unusually cooperative and expert assistance to the book's production. Deb Hoskins helped me to see how a new generation sees the subject.

There would have been no book without Esther Stillman Thelen. There might have been a book without Jennifer and Jeremy, even an earlier one, but it would have lacked its point.

Bloomington
November 1985

I

Gilded Age America and the Making of a Popular Politician

1855–1891

As veteran congressmen scrutinized the freshmen legislators who took their oaths of office in December 1885, they would have found nothing particularly unusual about the new member from Wisconsin's Third District, Robert Marion La Follette. His background was similar to that of many congressmen before him. Thirty years old and the youngest member of the Forty-Ninth Congress, he was perhaps a little more ambitious than many of his colleagues. At five-foot-five, he was a little shorter than most, but his luxuriant moustache hardly distinguished him from others. Like most congressmen from the upper Midwest, he had never questioned that the Republican Party uniquely fitted the nation's needs or that the opportunity to rise from rags to riches made the United States the finest civilization the world had ever known.

Faith in the American dream of opportunity came early to Robert M. La Follette. He was born on June 14, 1855, to a family whose ancestors had been moving steadily westward for a century in search of better land and more money. His parents lived five years in Primrose Township, Wisconsin, before the future senator was born, converting their wilderness into one of the township's most prosperous farms. But just eight months after Robert's birth, disaster struck; his father died. For the second time in a decade, Mary La Follette buried a husband, but this time she had four children to support. She turned the farm over to her son-in-law, who began to sell butter commercially, making her home even more prosperous. In 1862, when Robert was seven, she married John Saxton, a seventy-year-old wealthy merchant from a town twenty miles from the Primrose farm. Robert spent the next eight years of his life in the home of this smalltown merchant. By the time he was fifteen, when declining health and tough competition drove his stepfather out of business, he was ready to run the family farm and moved his mother and stepfather back to Primrose. La Follette, as a teenaged farmer, fully understood the rural westerner's dream of opportunity.

Even though the dream of riches might keep a man plowing and harvesting his fields from dawn to dusk, he needed other things to sustain him. Living long distances apart, La Follette's neighbors looked forward eagerly to all social gatherings, whether church sings, community dances, school in the winter, or chats with neighbors. Young La Follette shared this sociability with his neighbors, becoming an unusually outgoing person who loved to be with other people. He learned enough Norwegian to talk with his neighbors of that nationality. With his sensitivity to people and to social situations came an acceptance of the prevailing beliefs of others. He rejected his mother's Democratic Party because most of his neighbors were committed Republicans.

One prevailing belief that La Follette did not accept was evangelical religion, an important influence on the rural West. Evangelical religion held that the individual's responsibility was not only to live a moral life but also to try to abolish the sins of others. The community should use persuasion and social pressure against a neighbor who drank too freely, use laws against parochial schools which taught different standards of conduct, and even wage war against the

South for its arrogant efforts to carry its sin of slavery to the North and West. Robert La Follette's mother and stepfather were devout evangelical Baptists who entertained the minister every Sunday. Young La Follette would have easily absorbed this religious perspective had his mother not constantly insisted that he always revere the memory of his natural father who had died before his first birthday. His stepfather repeatedly charged that La Follette's father was roasting in hell for his agnostic views. Deeply resenting his stepfather's charge (as well, perhaps, as the old man's impatience with his playful stepson), young La Follette rejected the evangelical religion of his home and community.

In contrast, as he grew up Robert La Follette never questioned his family's and his neighbors' faith that education, or more precisely schooling, would create a brighter future by providing opportunities for the individual's moral and economic improvement. Mary La Follette shared this faith. She encouraged her youngest son to attend the district school at the age of four. In 1867 and 1869 she sold parts of the Primrose farm so that her children could attend private and presumably better schools that would prepare them for a better life than she had lived.

After four years of running the family farm, La Follette and his mother decided to stake the family's future on their ambitions for him. By 1873 Primrose was no longer very attractive. Saxton had died the year before; Robert's older brother had moved further west; and farm prices were falling fast. La Follette, his older sister Josephine, and his mother moved to Madison so that he could attend the University of Wisconsin. But before he could enter he had to spend two years taking preparatory courses to make up for the educational deficiencies of his rural background. Finally, in 1875, he was ready.

Most of the students at the University of Wisconsin came from farms and saw college as the avenue toward careers in law, medicine, engineering, and business. Dreaming of brighter futures than their farms offered, they rejected the farm protest movement that was sweeping Wisconsin in the mid-1870s and instead joined the Republican Party, which they associated with their rags-to-riches goal. They knew that entering college gave them a great advantage over others, for there were fewer than 27,000 college students in the United States when La Follette enrolled. In the spirit of sacrifice exalted in the American dream of rising from rags to riches, they expected to work to support their studies. La Follette paid for part of his education by teaching school in nearby towns and by selling books. His mother sold eighty more acres from the farm and took in boarders.

To finance his education, La Follette became publisher and editor of a student newspaper during his last three years in college. By employing freshmen at low wages and by industriously canvassing Madison's merchants to advertise, he earned about $700 each year. The paper endlessly eulogized the self-made man. It warmly praised *Self-Raised; or from the Depths,* by Mrs. E. D. E. N. Southworth, condemned reformers in the Democratic Party as shiftless ne'er do wells, and lambasted the tramps who wandered the Wisconsin countryside after the depression of the mid-1870s had thrown them out of work: "Let these heartless wanderers whose oaths taint the purity of the country air, claiming that the world owes them a living, be placed at such work and in such confinement that they will soon learn to follow a regular employment."

La Follette was mainly interested in the social aspects of college, and his natural sociability made him popular. "Let the music begin and the 'sound of revelry' be heard once more," he wrote, "or college life will lose its charms." He was the leading prankster on campus. Preferring any social contact to the lonely memorization of textbooks, he was a poor student. When called on to recite, he would often rise, shake his head, and sit down again. Half the faculty voted not to graduate La Follette, and only the tie-breaking vote of President John Bascom gave him his bachelor's degree in 1879. His mind was on extracurricular activities.

The Athenaean Literary Society gave him the forum for acting and speaking. Here students shared the "firm sympathy and friendship" of their brother members, as they gathered every Friday night to practice debate and oratory. La Follette preferred oratory to debate, and by the time of his graduation in 1879, he had won a reputation as one of the best orators in the Madison area.

Loving popular acclaim, he yearned to become a great actor whose characters would bring laughter, tears, and applause from audiences. As a child he had loved to entertain Saxton's customers by performing atop crates in his stepfather's store. He appeared frequently in plays, and finally channelled his need for public acclaim from acting to oratory only because a great Shakespearean actor told him that he was too short to be a convincing villain.

His dramatic instincts made him a great orator. The Athenaeans observed the sudden transformation that overcame La Follette as he mounted a stage. "The minute he got on the platform he became the actor," one of them recalled. His dramatic instincts honed the phenomenal sense of timing, vivid imagery, deep-throated intonation, and ability to take audiences through hell to a catharsis that made him such an effective orator. Athenaeans were not surprised by the crowning jewel of his oratorical career: they proudly joined the hundreds of Madisonians who jammed the state's Assembly Chamber on May 10, 1879, to celebrate La Follette's victory in the Interstate Oratorical Contest. The judges had voted him the best orator among 10,000 college students in the Midwest.

The young orator used the platform to tell people what they wanted to hear; his message was seldom novel. As a freshman, he had tried to please older Athenaeans by attacking the new fraternities that were challenging the literary societies. For the next twenty years he championed causes that his friends and neighbors advocated. In addition, he laced his rhetoric with a long moralistic and judgmental streak common among Gilded Age orators and encouraged by University President John Bascom and his evangelical environment. La Follette could turn public issues into a battleground between Truth and Falsehood, Black and White. But he saved his moralistic streak for the platform, where audiences wanted it. When he stepped down from the stage, he was again the outgoing warm person who charmed people easily.

Although he always liked to be with people, he was especially attracted to one classmate, the charming Belle Case, his future wife, who was five years younger than he was. Quietly ambitious, she was an excellent student who in 1885 would become the first woman graduate of the University of Wisconsin law school. She hated behavior or institutions that blocked the natural fulfillment of human spontaneity, and thus she attacked the artificiality of constricting Victorian dress and a male-only suffrage. During their courtship and marriage La Follette came increasingly to seek her approval and advice. She was his conscience at times when his easygoing sociability left him prey to others' ideas. They became engaged at the end of their junior year.

The couple needed an income before they could marry, so they decided that after graduation Belle would teach school in her home community of Baraboo and La Follette would become a lawyer. He took courses at the law school in the fall of 1879, read and discussed law in the office of a prominent attorney, and watched trials in Madison's courts. This proved training enough for him to pass the bar examination and be admitted to practice in February 1880.

Belle and Robert decided that he could best launch his legal career as district attorney of Dane County. The job paid $800 a year and traditionally went to young lawyers; it brought enough public recognition for one to build a private practice later. La Follette combined his local popularity as an orator and a charming young man with an understanding of political methods that came from his family's tradition as local politicians. He gave speeches in small towns around Madison on such nonpartisan topics as Shakespeare's Iago and on the evils of tramps. He shook as many hands as he could. He refreshed the Norwegian he remembered from his childhood. The Republican county politicians nominated him because he had proven his popularity and because they desperately needed to ditch an incumbent whose alcoholism and friendship with prostitutes were liabilities to the whole ticket. La Follette was elected easily along with the rest of the Republican ticket in the November general election, and he had no trouble winning renomination and reelection in 1882. During his first term he could finally afford to marry Belle Case.

He was a popular district attorney because he zealously prosecuted tramps, vagrants, drunkards, and other public nuisances. These shiftless wanderers offended both the temperance advocates and the people with faith in the mystique of the self-made man, the two main groups of GOP constituents. But he balked at the evangelicals' demand that he go beyond the prosecution of public nuisances to close saloons on Sunday. During the spring of 1884, when the Madison Law and Order League battled the Personal Liberty Society on this issue, La Follette retreated to a sickbed, finally emerging to engineer a compromise that ended the prosecutions. He had trained his sights on a higher post than the district attorneyship, and he wanted to disengage himself from a political controversy based on ethno-religious differences. He repeated this pattern for the rest of his life, for though he recognized the importance of ethno-religious affiliations for many voters, he would not offend others by committing himself to any one group.

As La Follette began to campaign for a higher office in the summer of 1884, he understood that big businessmen had captured control of the Republican Party leadership during his four years as district attorney. Frightened by the farmers' protest movements of the mid-1870s, which had produced railroad regulation laws, a group of businessmen, headed by lumber and railroad magnate Philetus Sawyer, seized control of the party's top leadership positions. They stripped Madison

Postmaster Elisha W. Keyes of his party chairmanship in 1877, defeated his bids for the Senate in 1879 and 1881, and finally took away his postmastership. La Follette knew that by 1884 he would need to work with the victorious group.

The victors were rich whereas Keyes had been poor, but equally important, they had a different ethno-religious strategy. The new businessman-politicians were secular and pragmatic. Because evangelical groups of Yankees and Norwegians would never vote Democratic, they reasoned, the party should concentrate instead on winning the support of the state's large German Protestant population, which switched its loyalties from one election to the next. The new leaders increasingly rewarded such nonevangelical groups with patronage and legislation.

La Follette understood these changes when he decided to run for Congress in 1884. To manage his campaign he sought out his old friend, Civil War General George E. Bryant, who had replaced Keyes as Madison postmaster; Bryant wanted a candidate who could create Republican harmony in the district that had elected a Democrat in 1882, when Keyes had split the Republican votes by running as an independent. La Follette tried to reach as many voters in the southwestern Wisconsin district as possible, and Bryant secured him the support of veterans, of farmers, and of politicians. La Follette considered Bryant his "political godfather," and he was a good godfather indeed. The young man won both the nomination and election with ease. (So tightly had he tied his campaign to Bryant that Democrats plausibly charged that "the Madison postmaster will be the real congressman.")

In 1885, La Follette became the youngest member of Congress. He and Belle never felt quite at ease with the special seasons and rhythms of Washington life. They moved from one boarding house to another. The young congressman thrust himself deeply into his work and enjoyed the feeling of power that accompanied his conversations with older Washington hands, but his wife, with her distaste for unnatural things, yearned for their home in Madison.

Within the House itself he made many friends. He admired the caustic wit and personal charm of "Czar" Thomas B. Reed from Maine and the affable and earnest William McKinley. He accepted his disappointing initial appointment to the Indian Affairs Committee without complaint and was delighted when Reed, impressed by his attack on Democratic Speaker John Carlisle, appointed him to the prestigious Ways and Means Committee. Despite his friendships with House leaders, La Follette authored no major laws, introduced few bills, and largely let others define the issues.

In 1885 La Follette began to build the foundations that would assure his reelection in 1886 and 1888. Eager to avoid the conflicts that were dividing more established Wisconsin Republicans, he built a very personal organization instead of depending on the party. He asked a friend in each ward and township in his district to compile lists of active Republican workers and open-minded Democrats who might campaign for him in the future. He sent copies of his speeches and free garden seeds to these people and tried to see them on each visit home. When Republicans regained the White House in 1889, he secured their appointments as postmasters or census enumerators. In return, they headed off rival candidates and worked for his reelection in the general campaigns. By placing his political fate in the hands of people personally dedicated to him, he was less dependent on established party organizations than most congressmen. At the same time, he had to pay particularly close attention to the wishes of his constituents.

Depending on direct contacts with voters, La Follette became the spokesman for his constituents. He introduced petitions from the Woman's Christian Temperance Union, and he favored bills to increase pensions for the Union veterans who had fought against the sinful South. But he carefully refused to state his position on liquor issues in his reelection campaigns.

La Follette reflected his constituents even better in his views on sectional and racial issues, arguing that the South, in trying to export its immoral racial discrimination, was trying to rob the North of its victory. He was "shocked by the public announcement from the South that this is a 'white man's government,' and startled to find the doctrine defended where it should be denounced and abominated."

Southern disfranchisement of blacks was "the last conspiracy of a too often disloyal people against their Constitution and their country," La Follette declared. The white South was subverting representative government by depriving the black citizen of his ballot, which to La Follette was "his defense, his power, his shield, his sword, his hope, his prophecy." La Follette vigorously supported black Republican candidates from the South who charged that they had been denied their seats in Congress because of white election frauds. He loudly championed the Force Bill of 1890 which would have employed federal officials to guarantee a free, unintimidated ballot to both races in the South. Washington's black community sensed that La Follette's support ran deeper than the ordinary interest of GOP politicians, and he was asked to address the graduating class of Howard University Law School in 1886.

La Follette's basic attitude toward race relations reflected the self-made man's faith in the small-scale capitalism of the West. The fundamental sin of the white South was that it denied blacks the opportunity to become farmers or merchants, to participate fully in the American dream. La Follette thus found a receptive audience among black leaders like Booker T. Washington, because they believed that the fundamental problem was to teach industrial discipline to freedmen and that this was impossible without economic opportunity. Blacks would have progressed economically and morally beyond immigrants, La Follette argued, if they "had been fairly treated, if they had received kindly recognition, if they had been provided with schools and books and teachers, if they had been given an opportunity to make homes for themselves, if their labor had been properly rewarded," if, in short, they had been given the rewards that would encourage them to acquire industrial discipline.

Opportunity was the key to the dream, and La Follette repeated his conviction that opportunity was what made American civilization the finest in the world. No hereditary aristocracy, arbitrary government, or dictatorial church limited the American's chance to advance. "Here the limitations upon the intellectual growth and development, the social place, and the financial success and triumph of each person are fixed by his own character and power alone," declared Congressman La Follette in 1890. "I care not what his birth or station, though born to an inheritance of poverty and toil and obscurity, if he be capable, if he be honest, if he be industrious, if he have courage and pluck and persistence, he will win wealth and power and honor and fame [because] all around him lies inviting and unlimited opportunity."

Believing deeply that America's greatness lay in its abundance of opportunity, La Follette favored economic programs that would promote even greater opportunities. He championed federal subsidies for agricultural experiment stations because research would stimulate farmers not to accept their present condition as the limit of their future opportunities. As farmers learned how to make more money from the scientists at the stations, their days would increasingly "be filled with mental exercise, made still more zestful with increasing profit." He strongly supported the Republican philosophy of tariff protection for American products not only to preserve the high standard of living of American workers but also to encourage the development of new products that would diversify the economy and thus create greater opportunities. He fought particularly hard for a high duty on flax because he thought that it would offer riches for farmers who had suffered economically for their dependence on wheat and cotton.

La Follette idealized the successful businessman. Men achieved success, he believed, because they worked harder, thought more clearly, and behaved more morally than their competitors. His constituents, who grew up with the legend of opportunity, expected politicians to behave in the same frugal way as the successful businessman. The trouble came, said La Follette, when politicians forgot "sound business principles" in their eagerness to win government expenditures for their districts. Other congressmen were more interested in getting a piece of pork for their districts than in developing a national plan for the best development of rivers and harbors to stimulate economic opportunities. He repeatedly lambasted rivers and harbors expenditures as "petty jobbery."

La Follette's faith in the self-made man assumed the existence of an open, competitive society in which an individual's abilities alone would determine his success. The key, La Follette believed, was an environment of competition and maximum opportunity. During the late 1880s, however, he began to see that competition was disappearing. Businessmen were investing more money in expensive, large-scale machinery and could no longer afford the instability of frequent rate wars. They were forming pools and trusts to prevent competition.

Although he saw clearly that a few corporations were subverting competition, La Follette still believed that the basic thrust of nineteenth-century America was to liberate the individual and that once the unnatural pools and trusts were abolished, history could resume its normal course toward competition. He cheered the section of the Interstate Commerce Act of 1887 that outlawed railroad pools because that section was "a declaration of the fundamental principle of law that agreements in restraint of trade and competition are against public policy." He warmly supported the Sherman Anti-Trust Act of 1890, believing that the act's prohibition of conspiracies in restraint of trade was a restatement of common law. He championed the Interstate Commerce Commission in 1887 because the new body would "remove the artificial restrictions that hinder the natural operation and course of trade and traffic."

Congressman La Follette understood the interest groups that descended on the capitol when Congress met. Many Americans followed the traditional pattern of forming job-based pressure groups to seek support from government, because they realized that in a representative system of government legislators needed ways of knowing what would be popular with their constituents. The interest groups then sent lobbyists to inform legislators how the dairy farmers, railroad workers, or small bankers in their districts would react to a specific bill. Legislators like La Follette had to know the relative size and influence of groups in their districts, and they had to decide the degree to which the constituents identified politics with their ethno-religious backgrounds or with dreams of future wealth, as well as with their jobs.

La Follette was so eager to please people and so sensitive to the wishes of his constituents that he often did not need lobbyists to tell him what was popular at home. He was, as one newspaper reported in 1890, "the steadfast friend of every interest in his district." First came the dairy farmers, the best-organized pressure group in the state. During the 1880s meat packers began to manufacture large amounts of oleomargarine to compete with butter. La Follette bitterly condemned oleomargarine and demanded that the federal government tax it out of existence. "Ingenuity, striking hands with cunning trickery, compounds a substance to counterfeit an article of food. It is made to look like something it is not; to taste and smell like something it is not; to sell for something it is not, and so deceive the purchaser. It follows faithfully two rules: 'Miss no opportunity to deceive;' 'At all times put money in thy purse.' " In short, oleomargarine was a "monstrous product of greed and hypocrisy." Dairy farmers thanked him. Wisconsin also was a leading wool-producing state; and the Third District led the nation in the growth of cigar-leaf tobacco. La Follette pushed hard for high tariffs against foreign competition to these products.

The popular La Follette would have had no trouble winning reelection to a fourth term had it not been for an earth-shaking battle in Wisconsin that produced a Democratic land-slide in 1890 and retired six of the state's seven Republican congressmen. The Republican faction elected in 1888 had secured a law that prohibited the labor of children under thirteen and required all between seven and fourteen to attend schools where instruction was given in English for at least twelve weeks a year. Some supporters of the measure wanted to recreate the Puritan community, in which everyone appreciated the importance of piety and the prevailing morality. Others believed that education was the avenue for mobility and that the schools inculcated the necessary values of hard work, thrift, punctuality, and temperance. By forcing children to learn English, both groups hoped to destroy the ethnic cultures that exalted other values.

German Lutherans and Catholics saw the law as a menace to their basic habits. They interpreted it as an attempt to destroy their culture by destroying their language and their schools and by imposing alien disciplines of punctuality and temperance. Realizing that Wisconsin had a higher proportion of immigrant voters than any other state in 1890, they thought that they could repeal the law. They captured the Democratic Party, and Catholic and Lutheran clergymen turned their parishes into branches of the party. After the Democrats had captured most state and national offices in the election, the 1891 legislature hastily repealed the hated law.

Congressman La Follette, as a loyal Republican, perfunctorily endorsed the law, but he devoted his reelection to other, and to him more important, issues. He was proud of his part in framing the McKinley Tariff of 1890, and he campaigned hard on it. He was still a popular orator, drawing large crowds, and he still spoke for the majority's sentiment on economic issues in the Third District. By appealing to his constituents' common identities as farmers and workers who would benefit by a high tariff, La Follette probably lessened some of the intensity of the ethno-religious conflict. But, in the end, that conflict was too much for the Republican Party, and he joined most of its candidates in defeat. He was only thirty-five at the time and hoped that Republican voters in the future would remember the epitaph of his congressional career offered by the district's leading newspaper: "No Wisconsin member in the history of the state ever made such rapid strides and gained so much prominence and influence in Congress. He was clearly the leader of [Wisconsin's] House delegation, although the youngest member from the state." La Follette moved the family back to Madison and threw all his attention to his law practice. Politics would wait for better times.

II

The Making of an Insurgent
1891–1900

THE POPULAR LEGEND of how ex-Congressman La Follette became an insurgent progressive gives credence to Napoleon's famous dictum that history is the agreed-upon myth. In 1911 friends and enemies alike considered La Follette the nation's oldest and most courageous progressive, and they readily accepted the account that he wrote in his autobiography that year. He described his life as a constant struggle against special interests and depicted the offer of a bribe in 1891 as the point at which he had resolved to convert the state of Wisconsin to progressivism. By 1900 he had accomplished his goal when Wisconsin voters, inspired by his speeches, elected him governor.

In fact, however, when the 1890s began, La Follette was a more or less typical politician whose main distinguishing quality was his receptivity to the mood and feelings of voters. When the economic depression that began in 1893 generated widespread popular unrest in Wisconsin and elsewhere and led voters to demand changes, La Follette sensed the popularity of insurgency — of challenges to privilege and concentrated wealth and power — and saw in it an opportunity to advance his career. When he began to champion insurgent measures in 1897 it was not as a longtime progressive but as a politician who was unusually responsive to grassroots attitudes.

La Follette never could have imagined these developments in 1891 when he settled into the life of a lawyer in Madison, Wisconsin. University students and state employees gave Madison a more intensely political and intellectual climate than that of most villages. Madisonians came to like their short, clean-shaven ex-congressman who worked so hard that he would annually collapse from nervous exhaustion.

During the 1890s he turned his mighty talents for zealous oratory to the courtroom and was soon the state's best jury lawyer. When La Follette won damages for a client who had lost a hand in an industrial accident, the defeated corporation lawyer angrily recalled that La Follette "could not have made humanity's case any more desperate if it had been the hand of Providence that was lost." Juries, like one considering a murder case, could not resist him:

> All of the dramatic art of La Follette, now shaking an index finger at a witness, now half sitting upon the reports' table, now with a point in hand by the map on the wall — La Follette, ever restless, ever eager — always in deadliest earnest, had set his stage scenery. Now his face was calm — now a thunder cloud — now full of sorrow. Here his voice arose almost to a shriek — there it sank to a whisper. . . . It was the artist in the orator, painting the colors on the words as they sprang from his soul. (*Wisconsin State Journal,* 1900)

Both La Follette and Belle liked to live the good life that included a farm as well as a city house, travel as well as the theater. They always needed money. Like Horatio Alger's virtuous but poor heroes, La Follette expected wealthy people to support him. During the 1890s he eagerly solicited the railroads' huge legal business in Madison. He received large annual retainers from the Milwaukee Railroad and defended it against charges of negligence by passengers and workers. Like other railway lawyers, he received free transportation for his family from the state's railroads. Later he sought help from wealthy progressives. He also invested in a horse ranch, an apartment building, a mine, and a telephone company in the hope that one would yield riches.

Family life was very important to both Robert and Belle La Follette. Their first child, Fola, was born in 1883, and for the next eleven years Robert's mother lived with them. When his mother died in 1894, La Follette became depressed. He and Belle decided that more children might compensate for the loss. Their second child, Robert Marion, Jr., was born in 1895, and he was followed in 1897 by Philip Fox and in 1899 by Mary. Fola, who was much older than the others, helped take care of the three young ones. Philip was an energetic irrepressible boy; Robert, Jr., tended to be silent and moody.

The La Follettes talked often about politics, and the children were always welcome at grown-up discussions. They all grew up to be intensely proud of their father, and they knew everything he was doing. When the family relaxed with a few close relatives and old college friends, La Follette would entertain them with his reenactment of classical plays and his readings in different dialects.

La Follette could not return to the state capital and expect to retire from politics. He gladly spoke for the ticket when Republican leaders asked him. He cherished the applause of the audiences, and he met — and charmed — dozens of politicians as he travelled all over the state to promote the party. Now, however, there was a difference in his relationship to the leaders — a difference that had grown out of a conversation he had on September 17, 1891, with United States Senator Philetus Sawyer. As he answered Sawyer's summons to Milwaukee's Plankinton House, La Follette knew that the senator would lose $300,000 if he lost a case that was about to be heard before La Follette's brother-in-law, Judge Robert Siebecker, in Madison.

What they actually said to each other must remain a mystery forever since Sawyer and La Follette told radically different stories. La Follette dashed home to Madison and told his family and friends that Sawyer had flashed a large roll of bills and promised more if La Follette could persuade Siebecker to decide the case "right." La Follette recalled that he had angrily told Sawyer: "If you struck me in the face you could not insult me as you insult me now." La Follette then told this story to Siebecker, who promptly withdrew from the case. Editors speculated that someone, probably Sawyer, had tried to bribe Siebecker. Sawyer immediately released his version. Sawyer explained that he had not known that Siebecker was La Follette's brother-in-law and was only trying to retain La Follette to help the defense lawyers.

The public battle between La Follette and Sawyer seriously affected La Follette's ambitions. Party leaders insisted publicly that the controversy was insignificant, but La Follette knew that the leaders closest to Sawyer would never forgive him for raising the whole issue. If he were ever again to run for office, he would need a personal organization.

Even during the 1880s he had relied for his elections on loyal friends and his zealous defense of popular causes more than on party leaders. In the 1890s, when he emerged as the leader of a new faction within the Republican Party, he again built a personal organization and championed popular issues as he sought to wrest control of the state party from Sawyer. His organization, like others across the country, battled the dominant faction only because it did not promote ambitious politicians rapidly enough. Reaching for power, they charged that wicked bosses controlled the ruling "machine" and pledged to throw the rascals out, while differing very little on matters of principle. Victory meant only that a different group would administer the state and distribute the patronage. There was nothing very reformist about La Follette's faction before 1897.

Although La Follette had alienated Sawyer's friends, other politicians turned to him because he was a "rattling campaigner" and charming person. "One can't shake hands with the man without a quiet feeling that he can get on the payroll any time he pleases," observed one editor. La Follette spoke at school picnics, county fairs, and church gatherings. In sharp contrast to the leaders of the ruling faction, he sought direct contact with voters.

He attracted individuals and groups with grievances against the "machine" — the Sawyer faction. Ambitious young men who thought they could rise faster in his organization than in the machine's joined him. Dairy farmers, who hated the machine for its subservience to the oleomargarine interests, also turned to La Follette, and their statewide leader, ex-Governor William D. Hoard, became one of La Follette's leading champions. In fact, dairy farmers colored his organization so completely in 1896 that one editor urged La Follette to learn that "there are more momentous issues involved in the present campaign than the dairy cow."

Scandinavians, living mainly in the rural western part of the state, had overwhelmingly supported the Republican Party since its formation and believed that the machine took their loyalty too much for granted and denied them long overdue political recognition. In the election of 1890, Sawyer and Henry C. Payne, who courted German Protestants, believed that Governor Hoard and the Republican 1889 legislature had blundered badly by sponsoring the school language law. Hoping that the Germans would soon return to the GOP, the machine leaders gave Hoard and the party only lukewarm support. Since Scandinavians did not particularly care about the law, they interpreted the machine's inaction in 1890 as proof of its indifference to them and preference for Germans. La Follette recognized the Scandinavians' desires and rewarded them. He chose Norwegian-born Nils P. Haugen as his organization's first gubernatorial candidate in 1894 because "I knew [the Scandinavians] felt a certain national pride in Congressman Haugen's prominence and success, and I counted on their giving him very strong support." La Follette wooed Scandinavian voters further by urging friendly state and federal officials to appoint Scandinavians to patronage jobs.

After the machine beat Haugen in 1894, La Follette and his friends began planning for 1896. La Follette decided to run for governor himself. He mailed more than a thousand letters to local politicians, most of them young, urging them to pack their caucuses with voters who would elect La Follette delegates to the state nominating convention. Ex-Governor Hoard appealed directly to voters to support his friend. La Follette was delighted with the results. He would go to the Milwaukee convention on August 5 with twelve more delegates than he needed to win the nomination.

Sawyer's friends had one thing La Follette lacked: money. On the night before the convention would nominate its governor, twenty delegates told La Follette that they had been offered bribes to support the machine's candidate. The next day the convention chose Edward Scofield.

La Follette's loyal delegates, many of them participating in politics for the first time, were furious. Though they urged him to run as an independent, La Follette knew that he could not possibly win. He sent the disappointed delegates home, determined to win in 1898. In the meantime, La Follette proved his loyalty by speaking for the entire GOP ticket in the fall.

In private, however, La Follette and his close friends brooded deeply over the 1896 defeat. As a responsive politician, La Follette began looking for issues to promote his candidacy for 1898. In 1897 he decided to advocate a program with which voters could associate him, one that fitted his own ambitions and style of popular politics. He took his new ideology directly from reformers who had been battling political establishments in towns and cities across Wisconsin and the nation. The obvious popularity of these grassroots reformers converted Robert M. La Follette into an insurgent progressive.

Insurgent progressivism drew together groups that had often fought during the nineteenth century. The common threat of large-scale enterprise drove them to submerge their differences. Believing that capitalism's basic virtue was its liberation of the individual to progress at his own speed and ability, devotees of the self-made man legend were restless and uneasy with the emergence of opportunity-limiting combinations of manufacturers and workers. Many evangelicals, disturbed enough by the greedy materialism that accompanied competition, grew positively alarmed by the development of huge soulless corporations that were impervious to conscience and morality. Long hostile toward the market economy that had undermined the preindustrial united community, many workers feared that the new, more complex, and more dangerous machines doomed them to a permanent, unsafe, and monotonous life as workers. In the desperate economic depression of 1893–1897, these groups found a common voice in insurgent progressivism, which incorporated their hatred of combinations, hostility toward materialism, and longing for a united community into a new tone of resentment toward large-scale industrialism.

The depression began in the spring of 1893 as a severe bankers' panic which caused more than one-fifth of Wisconsin's banks to fail in that year alone. The failures in turn bankrupted merchants, farmers, and manufacturers, and by the summer, the panic had broadened into a full-scale depression. By the winter of 1893–1894 more than a third of the state's workers could find no jobs, and unemployment continued high for the next three years. Desperate workers struck employers who cut their wages, and the unemployed marched on city halls and on Congress to demand relief. No one could escape the discovery that American capitalism was producing a large number of poor people.

Nor could anyone ignore the rich. Criminal prosecutions revealed that in at least six Wisconsin cities the bankers had been thieves and embezzlers. At this time of hardship, the lavish parties, fancy clothes, and expensive yachts of wealthy people seemed incredibly cruel. "The ostentation of the rich is a leading source of such discontent as we have among us," wrote a Milwaukee editor. The rich also seemed to have too much political power.

The appalling contrast between the rich and the poor severely challenged Americans to rethink their basic political beliefs. Some people felt compassion for their poorer neighbors: "Men are rightly feeling that a social order like the present, with its enormous wealth side by side with appalling poverty . . . cannot be the final form of human society," claimed a Methodist minister in Milwaukee. Others feared that the country would be destroyed by a revolution unless the gap between rich and poor were bridged. The country was developing Europe's unbridgeable gulfs between rich and poor, between privileged groups and the masses, between owners and toilers. The United States was no longer a middle-class democracy with unlimited opportunity for all. The discovery of social chasms challenged the deepest patriotism, for it threatened America's uniqueness.

It became very hard to believe that an individual's ability determined his social standing. Men and women failed to find jobs in the depression not because of any personal failing but because the economic system did not generate enough jobs. In this atmosphere of social unrest, the depression drove Americans to make common cause across the social barriers of age, nativity, occupation, and religion.

Neither ethnic leaders nor spokesmen for the economic interest groups were capable of meeting the depression's new challenges of tax-dodging and corporate arrogance. Most people's taxes remained at their predepression levels while the income to pay those taxes was rapidly declining. Many wealthy individuals and corporations, on the other hand, met the tax squeeze by hiding their stocks and bonds from the assessors and by lobbying tax relief through local and state governments and courts. The situation was critical in cities like Ashland, Wisconsin, where taxes were paid on only 57 per cent of the taxable property. By dodging their taxes, a few wealthy people had deprived the city of almost half the money necessary for schools, roads, sewers, firemen, policemen, and poor relief. Corporate arrogance affected people just as directly as tax dodging. Facing declining revenues, many corporations raised rates, lobbied special privileges through city and state governments, and refused to make improvements dictated by elementary considerations of health and safety. "Corporate arrogance" now meant epidemics of disease and death because the local water company, unable to afford to give residents healthful water, sent polluted, typhoid-infected water to homes and schools. It meant death to hundreds of Americans each year who were mangled and crushed under the wheels of streetcars because the traction company refused to install adequate bumpers on their cars. It meant higher lighting, power, transportation, and water bills for people whose incomes were declining.

Tax dodging and corporate arrogance thrust citizens into politics. Every ethnic and occupational group contained drinkers of death-dealing water, riders of unsafe streetcars, and users of utilities. They banded together to seek redress as taxpayers and consumers. When politicians failed to force companies to lower rates, to provide pure water, or to run safe streetcars, enraged citizens developed a new analysis of the political process. They learned that politicians were mostly interested in helping clearly recognizable ethnic or economic groups of voters. They also discovered that monopolistic businesses that performed public services had particularly intimate ties to politicians. These utility and railroad corporations had known from the start that their very existence depended on friendly relations with politicians, and they had appointed politicians to high management positions, supported them in campaigns, provided them with free services, and rewarded them (bribery was the more common term) for making policies favorable to the companies. Public service corporations and political leaders dominated the political process, and they formed a very tight establishment to resist grassroots pressures.

Angry taxpayers and consumers developed a new economic and political outlook to capture control of the political process: insurgent progressivism. Insurgency was rooted not in men's and women's social backgrounds — the ethnic, occupational, and religious identities that had motivated political cultures before 1893 — but in local problems that threatened everyone. Because the trauma of the depression was local and immediate — unemployed friends and family, death-dealing water from the home's faucet, increased streetcar fares, higher local taxes, criminal bankers in the community, bitter strikes at nearby factories, and declining income for everyone — the reaction was local and immediate. The only way to bridge the unsafe and unjust gulf between rich and poor and to stop corporate arrogance and tax-dodging was for men and women to band together across social divisions in their common roles as consumers, taxpayers, and citizens.

Since insurgent progressivism ran counter to men's and women's traditional tendencies to identify with their jobs or ethnic backgrounds, leaders searched for ways to reinforce the consumer-taxpayer-citizen framework. Attacking the greedy materialism of capitalism's competition among individuals, they championed the Golden Rule of love among neighbors regardless of background. "In the new society toward which we are now tending," declared an Appleton Presbyterian minister, "men will cease to compete against each other . . . and will co-operate with one another to make common cause, burying their mutual differences before a common foe." As insurgents came to agree with a state Congregationalist magazine that "there is no such thing as individual protection dissociated from mutual protection," they borrowed heavily from the ideal of the united community and its sense of mutual responsibility among all local residents.

Insurgents also built a new political outlook. The best way to prevent corporations from dominating city councils and state legislatures and to prevent pressure-group leaders and religious spokesmen from controlling elections was to give real political power to public opinion in the mass. Insurgents called this approach direct democracy, which meant giving the majority the power to initiate policy and rule directly. If the people directly nominated candidates for office by their votes in primary elections, no corporation-dominated ring, like Senator Sawyer's, could prevail. If the power to make laws and ordinances resided with voters at the polls, no lobbyists could reach powerful aldermen or legislators and frustrate rule by the majority. Insurgent progressives demanded that policy-making be returned to the local level, where citizens could more immediately control their destinies.

Behind the insurgents' drive to give the voter control over his political fate was the belief that public opinion supported them. If older politicians preferred the quiet of caucuses and legislative corridors, insurgent progressives relied on techniques of mass communication. They knew that the new — and truly popular — newspapers that sprang up in the 1890s reached citizens across social barriers. The editors of these newspapers often directed their sensationalist talents against local tax-dodgers and overbearing corporations. They firmly supported the insurgents' programs for tax reform, direct democracy, and social justice. Insurgents also rallied majority opinion with mass meetings, petition campaigns, reform leagues, and public lectures. The new agencies of mass communication, which transcended social backgrounds, would lead voters to reject their ethnic and job identities in favor of their common identities as consumers and taxpayers.

By the spring of 1897, as La Follette sought new issues, Wisconsin's insurgent progressives had proved the popularity of their programs. Insurgent mayors had been elected in Milwaukee, Janesville, Ashland, and Superior on their promises to tax the dodgers and regulate the corporations. At the state level, the insurgents, led by the Milwaukee Municipal League, had trebled utility taxes, repealed a special exemption law for utilities, and created a statewide commission to redistribute the tax burden. They had passed laws to nominate local candidates by direct vote instead of caucus action.

La Follette came to believe in 1897 that insurgent progressivism was the wave of the future. Sympathetic to majority views, he was also attracted to insurgent progressivism because it fitted his political style: he loved contact with mass audiences. La Follette had watched the insurgents use the issues of tax-dodging and corporation control of the political process to transform the machine into a popular villain. By 1897, Milwaukee's insurgent Republicans, including the mayor and several aldermen, had declared independence from Henry C. Payne because he had prostituted the Republican party to his public-service corporations. When La Follette took up the insurgent cause in 1897, the *Milwaukee Sentinel* accurately called him one of "the party leaders who try to find out what the popular current is, what the people want. . . . They may give effect to forces already at work and they may profit, too, by their recognition and understanding of these forces."

La Follette first promoted insurgency when he championed the direct primary in a speech at the University of Chicago in February 1897. Milwaukee had experimented briefly with such nominations in 1891, and most insurgents believed that corporations could not dominate local politics if candidates were chosen directly by the voters. La Follette reasoned further that the machine could never beat him again if the state adopted the direct primary. Sounding the insurgent note, La Follette cried: "Go back to the first principles of democracy; go back to the people."

When Chicago editors praised his solution to "The Menace of the Machine," La Follette raised money from friends like Hoard and printed 400,000 copies of a newspaper supplement that included his speech and a promotion for the Milwaukee Municipal League's corrupt practices act. During March and April more than 300 editors folded this free supplement into their papers. Racine Assemblyman William T. Lewis introduced a statewide primary bill, but legislators heeded the older insurgents, not La Follette. They enacted the corrupt practices act, in which La Follette had little interest, and established direct nominations in the state's fourteen largest cities, which insurgents wanted, while defeating the statewide primary bill.

After the legislature had adjourned, La Follette modified his program and strategy to fit the insurgent style more closely. He decided to take his program and his candidacy directly to the voters. From July 4, at Mineral Point, until September 24, at Milwaukee, La Follette spoke to audiences at county fairs across the state, arguing that he was the best man to implement the popular insurgent program. He told listeners that the cause of the "unsettled, restless condition of the public mind" in the depression was "the growing conviction . . . that we are fast being dominated by forces that thwart the will of the people and menace representative government." Those forces could be traced back to the rapid extension of the "powerful but invisible hand" of the modern, large-scale corporation.

Before the rise of the corporation, La Follette maintained, a businessman "gave his individuality, stamped his mental and moral characteristics upon the business he conducted." His consumers all came from the local community, and they patronized only the businessman who heeded their wishes for quality, safety, and integrity in products and services. But consumers could not discipline the modern, large-scale corporation. Each employee of the corporation "has become a mere cog in one of the wheels of a complicated mechanism" that "exacts but one thing of its employees: obedience to orders." Since "all individual responsibility, all business conscience is sunk in the impersonal, intangible entity of the corporation," consumers and the community could best restore their discipline over products and services by restoring competition.

After describing the virtual deathgrip that large corporations had over the nation's life, La Follette proposed his remedies. If citizens were to regain control over their lives, they had first to recapture the political process from the corporations, and the way to do this was through the direct primary. Appealing directly to angry taxpayers, he proposed to strip the railroads and other public service corporations of a special privilege they had enjoyed since 1854. Most individuals and businesses paid taxes on the basis of their physical property, but railroads and related corporations paid on the basis of income. This meant that these corporations could adjust their tax bills to the depression and could shunt the burden of taxes onto everyone else. Reflecting this unique privilege, the railroads had contributed 72 per cent of the state government's revenue on the eve of the depression but only 47 per cent by the time La Follette was speaking. Echoing the local insurgents, La Follette demanded that railroads and public service corporations pay taxes on the same basis as everyone else — their physical property.

As the campaign of 1898 approached, La Follette further developed his program and methods. In the fall of 1897 some friends bought him a weekly newspaper to take his views to the voters. He showed how public-service corporations dominated the political machine and betrayed public opinion: the Republican state government had rejected a proposal to outlaw free railroad transportation to politicians, a proposal that nearly 98 per cent of the voters had favored in an informal statewide referendum, because the leaders were too friendly to the railroads and needed free favors from the railroads for their own businesses. Governor Scofield had vetoed a law taxing express companies on the basis of their physical property in the summer of 1897 because an express company had shipped free his household goods, including a cow, from his Oconto home to the executive residence in Madison. Scofield's cow, La Follette cried, symbolized the railroads' domination over the "machine."

The machine leaders fought La Follette's candidacy bitterly. He was no longer just another ambitious politician who was challenging them for control of patronage jobs, but a dangerous demagogue who threatened to strip public-service corporations of their political power. Watching the rapid rise of insurgency at the local level, the public-service corporations and their political allies feared that reform would not stop with taxes but would continue until their businesses had been destroyed. They ordered railroad workers to vote against La Follette in the caucuses or lose their jobs. They spent $8300 to bribe delegates to the state nominating convention. And they renominated Governor Scofield.

Although the machine again defeated La Follette's bid for the governorship in 1898, the challengers forced the party to accept their planks in the platform and persuaded the delegates to nominate La Follette's friends for two lower statewide offices. La Follette reasoned that he could win in 1900 if he compromised with and divided the machine's leaders.

The machine cooperated. Sawyer was well past eighty years of age and would die before the 1900 convention. Senator John Coit Spooner preferred helping Nelson Aldrich run the Senate to aiding Sawyer in controlling Wisconsin. Republican National Committeeman Henry C. Payne spent 1899 in a last, desperate, and successful battle to save his Milwaukee streetcar and lighting monopoly from annihilation by that city's insurgents. By the time he had bribed a third of that city's aldermen, driven one alderman to suicide, defied a judge's injunction, and betrayed his party's platform to save his private utility, he had few friends left among Milwaukee Republicans and was powerless to prevent the party's insurgents from nominating one of their number for mayor in March of 1900. Sensing that La Follette and the insurgents would soon control the state party, the lesser machine leaders fought each other bitterly for the Senate seat that became vacant in 1899. Congressman Joseph Babcock and millionaire lumberman Isaac Stephenson fumed in anger when Milwaukee corporation lawyer Joseph Quarles won the post. Stephenson promptly turned over his huge bankroll to La

Follette to get revenge. With their leaders distracted, bickering, and dying, county and city politicians scurried aboard the La Follette bandwagon. The once-powerful machine was a hollow shell by 1900.

While the machine was falling apart, La Follette carefully strengthened his organization. Men in every precinct and township prepared lists of sympathetic voters and turned them out at the caucuses. Dairy farmers buttonholed local merchants, and the Scandinavians, sensing political acceptance at last, turned out in record numbers. When La Follette stopped his personal denunciations of machine Republicans and when the 1899 legislature enacted the antipass and partial tax planks in the 1898 platform, most of the state's Republican editors, who had long sympathized with his program but resented his personal attacks, declared that La Follette had earned the chance to be governor. La Follette and ex-Governor Hoard privately assured railroad officials that the candidate was less radical than he sounded on the platform. When the nominating convention met in August 1900, La Follette won without a contest. The platform praised President McKinley and Senator Spooner and advocated the direct primary, equal taxes, vague antitrust measures, and economy in government.

La Follette launched a vigorous campaign to beat Democrat Louis G. Bomrich in November. Wrapping himself in the cloak of McKinley's popularity, he developed Wisconsin's first whistle-stop campaign, which carried him 6433 miles in the last three weeks as he made 208 speeches to about 200,000 people. Riding the crest of Republican popularity, La Follette trailed McKinley by 1341 votes but won 60 per cent of the vote and carried 64 of the state's 70 counties, losing only in 6 heavily German and heavily Democratic counties.

III

The Insurgent as Administrator

1901–1905

THOUSANDS jammed the University of Wisconsin gymnasium on January 7, 1901, to shake hands with the new governor at his inaugural ball. La Follette's election, however, held different promises for different groups of people. It promised political acceptance to Scandinavians, relief from oleomargarine manufacturers and railroads to dairy farmers and grain merchants, curbing of utilities to local insurgents, and patronage to politicians. Each expected rewards for years of support, for now the insurgent candidate was the administrator and boss. On that cold January day none of them could imagine that La Follette would develop a unique brand of progressive leadership that promised rewards to all of them while making a full commitment to none.

Governor La Follette surprised all because he behaved in unfamiliar ways. La Follette had won his office by appealing to the specific grievances of particular groups and to the vague sense of powerlessness felt by taxpayers and consumers. He believed that he could best satisfy his supporters by securing a specific legislative program – the direct primary and the railroad tax law. Assuming that the best way to achieve that program was to continue the spirit of party harmony, he

reappointed incumbents to the major state boards and promoted party peace in his inaugural address. He hoped to win
legislative support by announcing in February that he would
defer the remaining appointments until after the legislature
adjourned, but supporters who expected immediate rewards
were furious. La Follette was forcing legislators to support his
pet bills before they would be rewarded. He seemed to be
rewarding enemies and punishing friends.

At the same time he baffled local insurgents by ignoring
their desperate cries for relief from oppressive monopolies. In
1901 South Milwaukee was fighting a flagrantly corrupt streetcar and lighting monopoly. Ashland in 1901 was fighting a
water company whose impure water caused a typhoid fever
epidemic that produced 500 cases of the disease and 30 deaths
by March. Insurgents introduced bills to reassert popular control over the hated utilities by requiring a popular referendum on franchises, by allowing cities to acquire debt for
public ownership, by taxing utilities on the same basis as other
property, and by permitting changes in the terms of franchises.
The local insurgents could not understand why La Follette
ignored their bills.

Ignoring politicians and local insurgents alike, La Follette
pressed ahead, confident that the overwhelmingly Republican
legislature would speedily adopt his two measures. But the
Federal faction, led by Senator John Spooner's 4684 Federal
officeholders in Wisconsin, would not be mollified by superficial gestures of harmony into supporting a direct primary.
They believed that party caucuses generated enthusiasm. Germans feared they would lose their veto over potential
nominees who would attack their cultural habits. Conservatives feared that direct nominations would entrench "demagogues" like La Follette whose success depended on attacking
corporations and private property. The railroads, eager to
bury the tax bill, encouraged legislative attacks on any part of
La Follette's program.

As criticism mounted, La Follette forgot harmony and

counterattacked. He directed state appointees to pressure local politicians. He charged that Republican legislators had forfeited their party membership by opposing the party's promises of a direct primary and tax reform. Many supporters urged him to compromise by accepting primary bills that would apply only to local nominations, would submit the law to a referendum, or would retain the state convention while abolishing caucuses. La Follette refused. He knew that he would be nominated by a direct primary, and he insisted that it apply to the governorship even if the compromise would have helped local insurgents. He had never been comfortable with the strategy of 1900 and early 1901 of cooperating with decade-old enemies. Now thwarted by these politicians when he tried to be easygoing and compromise, he reverted to moralistic oratory to expose the voters' enemies.

Compromise would be a sellout. He vetoed a direct primary bill that applied only to local nominations, charging that the legislature had not enacted a stronger law because "an array of federal officeholders, joining with certain corporation agents and representatives of the machine . . . , moved upon the capitol, took possession of its corridors, intruded into the legislative halls, followed members to their hotels, [and] tempted many with alluring forms of vice." And when the legislature buried his railroad tax, La Follette dramatized legislative indifference to poor taxpayers by vetoing a bill to tax dogs, crying that legislators would rather tax farmers' dogs than the powerful railroads. The Senate counterattacked, censuring La Follette by an 18-to-8 vote for rising above "all bounds of official propriety" in his charges. The issue was now fully joined.

La Follette developed a new conception of reform leadership. Local insurgents wanted to change policies, but La Follette wanted to win elections. He felt that his election and reelection were the most important progressive reform in Wisconsin. By voting for him, he insisted, the people gave "a full expression of their views" and allowed him to select any issues he wanted. Insurgent voters accepted this messianic and plebiscitarian concept of leadership because they believed, based on local experiences, that their leader would have to be a superman to defeat the corporations. Many insurgent voters were also willing to trust La Follette to choose the best means to terminate corporate arrogance because they lacked the ethnic and occupational allegiances that had traditionally motivated voters and shaped issues and because the state level was remote from their local communities where insurgent grievances had originated. "With Roosevelt for our national leader and La Follette bearing our state banner," wrote an educator from Stevens Point, "we of the ranks can fight with courage for the victory of right principle and honest government."

La Follette could thus select the issues. He had chosen the direct primary and railroad tax because local insurgents had already popularized them and because he could handle only two issues in his speeches. La Follette's decision to promote these at the expense of the traditional concerns of politicians angered old-style politicians who thought that a governor should be mainly concerned with patronage. Even arguments over the spoils of office thus became ideological battles. At the same time he angered local insurgents by ignoring issues other than the two he had decided to promote. Typhoid fever epidemics in Ashland or streetcar tax-dodging in South Milwaukee were irrelevant. He blocked Assemblyman Albert R. Hall's proposals for railroad rate regulation. He shunned a statewide lobby of local insurgents and city officials fighting utility arrogance, with the result that fewer insurgent bills passed in 1901 than had passed in 1897 or 1899 when governors had left the initiative to others. When a huge convention of farmers in February demanded tax reform, La Follette told them that the best method would be to support his primary bill.

Soon after the legislature adjourned in May, he collapsed. For nearly a year he suffered acute stomach pains and several times hung precariously near death. He had weighed 160 pounds on June 20; by September 23 he weighed 130. Doctors were baffled. Finally, in October, prominent Chicago physician Frank Billings pronounced that "the fundamental cause of his trouble is . . . an unbalanced nervous apparatus, the result of over-work, and in consequence a neurosis of the stomach." La Follette drove himself to the point of nervous exhaustion. He believed that victory in anything came only if one could anticipate and manage every detail of a problem. Belle reminded him that the preparation of a speech hung "over the household like a nightmare for months, seeming to wear out your nervous vitality with dread and anxiety." As one legislator after another opposed his program in 1901, La Follette had redoubled his fight. His collapse resulted from a conflict between his compulsion for perfection and his desire to please individuals. For the rest of his life his stomach paid the price; doctors allowed him to eat only granose biscuits, English walnuts, zwieback, butter, and milk.

The conflict that produced his collapse in 1901 had roots reaching back to his earliest childhood memories. His mother had insisted that he worship a father he had never really known. La Follette grew up wanting to know more about his idealized father in order to know what behavior would have pleased him. In his mid-twenties Robert La Follette dreamed, "I am standing beside my father's grave. Oh my idolized father lost to me before your image was stamped upon my child-brain — nothing left but your name! What would I not give to have known the sound of your voice, to have received your approval when it was merited." His relentless quest for information about his father even drove him to excavate his father's grave and carefully examine the relics of the skeleton in his hands. He began to worship older men who possessed the passion for right-doing that his mother had told him his father had and who could serve as authority figures — university president John Bascom, Madison Postmaster George E. Bryant — because they could give him the approval he so badly needed. Much of his passion to make a "record" that moral men would respect flowed from his need to please an idealized father he had never known.

Although he sought the approval of father figures, he also developed a profound distrust of men with power. He hated his stepfather, who had disciplined him as a child and had condemned his natural father to hell. Even father figures could never be completely trusted because they might suddenly die and leave a boy to the mercies of a wicked stepfather. Part of his distrust of the powerful stemmed from his childhood, when he came to believe that noble purposes and hard work, which he associated with his father, not raw power, which he associated with his stepfather, conferred legitimacy. He had begun his campaign against the machine in 1891 when a kindly father figure, Senator Sawyer, had tried to use the rawest form of power, bribery, and he had immediately placed the bribe on public record to show that this apparent father was actually a stepfather. As he drove himself ever harder, he became increasingly singleminded in his determination to make a record; his guts would coil tighter, he would lash out bitterly at his critics, and finally he would collapse from nervous exhaustion, his stomach pounding with pain. Many voters profoundly admired the governor who would fight to the point of collapse. They felt that he was suffering for them.

During the rest of 1901 and most of 1902, as he alternated between recovery and relapse, La Follette sought to vindicate his record with a triumphal reelection in 1902. Since the Republican party was bitterly polarized, La Follette decided to offset the loss of conservative Republican voters with gains from insurgent Democrats. The Federal faction accepted his challenge to battle over ideology. In August its leaders created an organization, bankrolled by corporations trying to escape higher taxes, to deny La Follette the renomination. Fifty-nine Republican legislators pledged that the new group would "discourage visionary, dangerous experiments in legislation which appeal to prejudice . . . and [injure] the reputation of the state for conservatism and sound business and political judgment." Voters who wanted any kind of reform had to choose La Follette.

La Follette realized that he needed the press if he was going to persuade voters to reject traditional appeals based on job, ethnic, and partisan identity and to support his issues. In 1901 he could depend on 112 smalltown papers. He persuaded the state's richest man, Isaac Stephenson, to join a few Milwaukee grain merchants in underwriting a newspaper with statewide circulation. On June 18, 1902, the *Milwaukee Free Press* began its daily attacks on the Federal faction for its subservience to public-service corporations. La Follette ordered his ward and township supporters not only to get out the vote but also to distribute literature and solicit subscriptions to the *Free Press*. To make certain that all voters had "a full knowledge of the momentous issues involved" he published 132,000 copies of a 144-page handbook that exposed corporate control over the legislature and described his plans for a direct primary and railroad tax to end that control.

La Follette's organization swamped the Federal faction at the caucuses. Controlling the state convention, La Follette insisted that ideology be the test of party fidelity. After nailing tax and primary planks into the platform, he announced that the platform was "a written contract deliberately entered into with every man who casts his vote for candidates of that party" which every Republican had to honor.

La Follette completed his ideological alignment of Wisconsin politics by making his issues, not traditional symbols, the basis of division between the two parties. The Democrats helped by nominating Milwaukee Mayor David Rose on a platform that opposed the railroad tax and direct primary. Since Rose had protected the Milwaukee Electric Railway and Lighting Company, which monopolized transportation, lighting, and power, from insurgent efforts to regulate and tax it, La Follette ordered his lieutenants to treat Rose "as the one man who could be found to do the dirty work of the Milwaukee Street Car monopoly." "Appeal to the citizenship of the state to save Wisconsin's good name from this gang of corporation knaves," he directed. "Arouse patriotic, not party feeling." La Follette believed with other insurgents that patriotic appeals could weaken the traditional job, ethnic, and partisan loyalties of voters.

His strategy worked. Voters in 1902 divided along ideological lines. Although his winning percentage declined, he carried all but nine counties. For every conservative Republican who voted for Rose, a "fair-minded Democrat" voted for the governor. In Kenosha County, for example, 29 per cent of the Republican voters selected Rose and 32 per cent of the Democratic voters chose La Follette. La Follette had succeeded in making his name synonymous with reform in both parties. His constituents were no longer the "Republican voters" he had championed in 1900. Now he spoke for "the people."

"The spirit of democracy is abroad in the land," La Follette told the 1903 legislature. The legislature accepted La Follette's interpretation of his reelection — that "the people" favored his plans for a direct primary and railroad tax — and enacted La Follette's direct-primary plan, subject to a referendum in 1904. Appealing to the taxpayers' revolt, La Follette's railroad tax law remedied one of the insurgents' oldest grievances. The state would hereafter tax the railroads as they taxed individuals and other businesses — on the basis of their actual property, not on their earnings. The new law raised the railroads' tax bill from $1,900,000 in 1904 to $3,400,000 in 1906.

La Follette also interpreted the 1902 election as popular support to strike out in any new directions he wanted. He surprised most voters in 1903 when he devoted much of his legislative message to a demand for railroad rate regulation, an issue he had previously ignored and one that was popular only with Assemblyman Albert R. Hall and the Milwaukee commission grain merchants.

La Follette's championship of railroad regulation marked

his evolution from a spokesman for long-popular causes to a leader who tried to popularize new issues. This evolution had many causes. He could not ignore the campaign for rate regulation begun in 1902 by his chief newspaper, the *Free Press*. He wanted to establish a record as a leading national reformer, and Wisconsin lagged badly behind most midwestern states in this area. He hoped that regulation would draw most of his opponents' fire and thus assure passage of the direct-primary and tax laws. Furthermore, he was aware that railroads were popular enemies because they dodged taxes, corrupted politicians, and were the first of the hated monopolies. Insurgent voters would applaud any victory over them.

After blasting the railroads for their prostitution of politics, La Follette claimed in his 1903 message that the new tax law would be a hollow victory if the railroads made consumers pay higher taxes in the form of higher freight rates. Rate regulation would mean lower prices to consumers because the railroad rate was "an important element in the cost of our clothing, our food, our fuel. It adds materially to the price of everything we purchase." In linking tax reform to lower prices, he showed insurgent voters that he understood their concerns as consumers, not just as taxpayers. He was trying to direct the widespread sense of consumer powerlessness to matters that were not so obvious as death-dealing water and to show how old issues — such as the clash between railroads and shippers — could be recast as consumer issues at the state level.

La Follette was totally unprepared for a fight in the 1903 legislature. The grain merchants and others gave him a quick course in the complexities of railroad rates, but he did not have a bill until March 6. In the meantime, those who profited from the existing rate structures had founded the Wisconsin Manufacturers' Association, an imposing lobby, to defeat regulation. They persuaded businessmen who depended on the railroads' good will to bury the legislature under antiregulation petitions. Administration legislators only dimly understood the technicalities. By April La Follette realized that his only hope lay in a direct appeal to the voters. Between April 23 and May 7 he sent three special messages to the legislature roasting the railroads for dodging taxes on secret, illegal rebates to favored shippers, for raising rates on the cost of coal to the state government, and for corruptly defeating the will of the people. The messages came too late. Regulation could only have passed in 1903, as Assemblyman Joseph M. Cowling observed, "if the matter had been agitated" earlier. La Follette now had his issue for 1904.

When the legislature adjourned, La Follette embarked on a new career that combined insurgency with income. From June 23 until September 2 he gave fifty-seven Chautauqua speeches in Wisconsin and other midwestern states, earning over $10,000. The Chautauqua performances, usually lasting about a week, formed the social highlight of the year for rural communities, combining entertainment with uplift, as they brought those communities out of isolation and into a national popular culture. As local Chautauqua committees increasingly tried to please their communities by inviting insurgent heroes like La Follette, William Jennings Bryan, and Denver's Ben Lindsey, Chautauqua progressivism played a major part in nationalizing a movement that had originated in local experiences, and its audiences helped to reward the insurgents financially.

As the campaign of 1904 drew closer, La Follette invented a new form of insurgent campaigning. He publicly read legislators' roll call votes. He went to the hometowns of legislators who had voted against his bills, orated on the need for railroad regulation, and then announced that the community's own representative had voted against it, implying that he was a tool of the railroads. La Follette's roll calls pointed toward a style of politics in which the sole test of a legislator's accountability to his constituency would be whether he voted for the governor's pet issues. He thus reinforced the image of him as the only true spokesman for the people and the image of anyone who disagreed with him for any reason as an enemy of the people.

His supporters among traditional politicians began to balk. "Like a pack of white-livered cowards," La Follette wrote a close friend, his supporters had refused to follow his February 1904 order to block Congressman Joseph Babcock's renomination. Noting that La Follette's growing insurgency was isolating him from politicians interested only in patronage, the *Chippewa Independent* shrewdly observed: "The chief trouble is that Governor La Follette believes in fidelity to campaign platforms and public pledges, while the Republican leaders . . . believe that all . . . campaign pledges should be disregarded to attain their particular wishes. The Governor is in about the condition of a hen with a brood of ducks. The parent and the brood speak different languages and have irreconcilable tastes."

Fearing that the refusal of some of his supporters to follow his command to contest Babcock's renomination presaged a crumbling of his faction, La Follette nervously awaited the results of the caucuses that would send delegates to the state nominating convention in May. He was horrified to discover that the Federal faction claimed, as did his supporters, to have elected a majority of the delegates. La Follette's State Central Committee responded by certifying only uncontested delegates and using a barbed wire barricade and football players to bar challengers from the convention. When the convention's first roll call established that the La Follette forces had an 89-delegate majority, a Federal delegate charged that the La Follette convention was illegal and announced that the Federal faction would hold its own convention that night. The Federal delegates declared themselves the official state convention, nominated S. A. Cook for governor, and selected their own delegates to the Republican National Convention to meet in June. Undaunted, La Follette's convention met the next day, promised railroad regulation, an income tax, and a law to end corporate lobbying, and renominated La Follette. Reflecting La Follette's insistence that ideology be the test of partisanship, both the platform and his acceptance speech emphasized the importance of platform pledges as "sacred obligations binding upon every member of the party."

The Republican National Committee then certified the Federal delegation, led by Senator Spooner, as the official one from Wisconsin. "The action of the national committee in Chicago," cried La Follette, "has made the Wisconsin fight a national issue." He would appeal over the heads of national politicians to Republican voters across the country "to rid the Republican party of corporation control and again make it the party that it was in the days of Lincoln."

In 1904, La Follette campaigned almost entirely by direct, mass appeals to voters and to a national reform constituency that could give him the legitimacy denied him by the national party leaders. He printed enough literature for every voter to receive four copies. "The verdict of the people will be right," he declared, if they could get the truth. His campaign boiled down to a struggle between "government of the people" and "government by public-service corporations. Around that vital issue the great political battles of the next twenty-five years will be fought out." A vote for La Follette was a vote for future national leadership. He entered legislative races by showing how the communities in which he spoke suffered from unfair rates, and, by reading the roll call on its representatives, he showed the community that it needed to elect a more responsive legislator.

La Follette also courted the new muckracking journalists and popular magazines, which he had previously ignored. Journalists like Samuel Hopkins Adams, Walter Hines Page, Ray Stannard Baker, Richard Lloyd Jones, Benjamin T. Flower, and Lincoln Steffens reported the Wisconsin campaign as La Follette desired. Baker was so impressed by La Follette that he and *McClure's* were ultimately and successfully sued for libel when they reprinted one of La Follette's

1904 campaign charges as though it were a fact. But it was Lincoln Steffens who really settled the issue in Wisconsin.

Steffens reported in a *McClure's* article in late September that Wisconsin was a state in which "the people have restored representative government." He observed that La Follette was indeed a "boss," but he was a boss dictating democracy. This article, La Follette wrote Steffens, "was like the decision of a court of last resort." Even his bitterest enemies realized that Steffens, not the state supreme court, which a few days later declared La Follette the official nominee, had decided the issue. But Steffens and the muckrakers had fulfilled an even deeper need for La Follette than his reelection: they had carefully examined his "record" and they approved it. With his own organization shaken, La Follette was becoming an issue-oriented insurgent who trusted the mass media more than his political organization.

After winning the nomination battle and, more importantly, the approval of the mass media, La Follette found the final returns of the 1904 election anticlimactic. Voters chose ideology over traditional party loyalties even more than they had in 1902. Although Roosevelt was carrying 63 per cent of the Wisconsin vote, La Follette only won 51 per cent. His loss of 53,000 conservative Republican voters was again offset by gains from "fair-minded Democrats." In addition to the usual Republican failure to carry German Democratic areas, La Follette did badly among the upper middle classes in the cities who, for the first time, began to perceive a real threat in his emerging ideology. Most observers joined the *Milwaukee Journal* in lumping La Follette's victory with those of Roosevelt and insurgent Democrat Joseph W. Folk in Missouri to argue that "one impulse has contributed alike to their success," for ideology was transcending partisanship across the country.

La Follette was gratified that 62 per cent of the voters had voted for the direct primary. The direct primary would further weaken partisanship and strengthen issue-oriented candidates who could appeal across job and ethnic divisions and knew how to use the new agencies of mass communication.

The first business of the 1905 legislature was to select a United States Senator. La Follette wanted the job in order to carry his cause to Congress, but he also wanted to remain governor to redeem the 1904 platform. Since he had prevented any of his lieutenants from acquiring independent stature, both he and his organization believed that he would have to accept both posts — governor and senator. This was the only way to stop his lieutenants from fighting each other and causing his pet bills to die and a conservative senator to be elected. In accepting the senatorship, he announced that he would not go to Washington until the legislature redeemed the 1904 platform.

La Follette tried hardest to redeem the rate-regulation plank. Railroad regulation, he told legislators, would bring fairer rates to small shippers and lower prices to consumers. It would limit the nearly absolute power of the six financial syndicates that owned the railroads and would expose their secret business and political activities. La Follette wanted to copy Texas's radical law that gave a commission the power to make rates on its own initiative without awaiting complaints. The railroads and their allies supported a commission that would act only on complaints, leaving initial rate-making power to the railroads. As a popular educator whose strength lay in raising broad issues of principle that divided the people from their betrayers, La Follette was poorly equipped to handle the gap between the principle of state regulation of railroad rates, which he had campaigned for and which everyone professed to accept, and the details of the bill, which he had largely ignored in his campaigns and which few legislators clearly understood. Sensing that some bill would pass and that La Follette had lost control of the details of the legislative situation, champions of a strong bill (including the grain merchants) began working with William H. Hatton, chairman of the Senate Railroad Committee. The final law reflected Hatton more than La Follette. It permitted the commission to act only on complaints, legalized the commodity rates that enriched the lumber barons, and compromised on the crucial issue of the courts' power to alter the commission's decisions. La Follette was tempted to follow the advice of radical advisers like Texas's S. H. Cowan to veto the bill and fight in 1906 to elect legislators who would vote for a strong bill. But since he wanted to enter the Senate, he joined Republican legislators in claiming that he had redeemed the platform by signing the bill.

La Follette's failure to secure a strong railroad law in 1905 revealed the problems in his special kind of reform leadership. Wisconsin had many well-organized groups of farmers, and La Follette had clearly understood and represented their particular grievances as a congressman in the 1880s. But by 1905 he was too interested in mass appeals to consumer-taxpayer consciousness to appeal to the interest groups that might have saved his strong bill. Instead of arguing that a strong railroad commission could help farmers or businessmen to secure cheaper rates for their products, he argued that it would help everyone as consumers. His special messages in April and May attacked the railroads for dodging taxes and killing passengers — two direct appeals to consumers and taxpayers — but he did not attack the railroads for hurting farmers and businessmen. Thus these groups, which might have helped him pass his bill, paid little attention to the railroad issue. Even his supporters in the Milwaukee Chamber of Commerce ignored him.

Another weakness in La Follette's style of politics involved his impatience with administrative detail. He preferred exposure, publicity, and election campaigns to the boring daily routine of administering laws and appointing officeholders. For this reason he championed the civil service reform act of 1905, hoping to free himself from the responsibility of making appointments.

He also paid little attention to the administrative innovations that overhauled the state tax structure while he was governor. After appointing one of his ablest lieutenants, Nils P. Haugen, to the State Tax Commission, he let that commission spearhead tax reform. He followed its advice for his railroad tax bills but carefully dissociated himself from its efforts to compel assessors to stop underassessing the value of property in their communities and to base their assessments on the actual selling price of real estate. La Follette saw only that the voters in grossly underassessed areas would be angry with the commission's actions, and he wrote his local lieutenants to isolate him from the increased assessments.

Governor La Follette's uncertainty about the best method for taxing wealth likewise reflected his tendency to let public opinion shape the specific forms of his programs. He realized that a taxpayers' revolt against wealthy individual and corporate taxdodgers was a basic fuel for insurgency, but he was uncertain where to proceed beyond the railroad tax. Like local insurgents, he wanted to devise a method to tax the increasingly invisible wealth of savings, mortgages, stocks, and bonds that escaped taxation. He shifted his position on the issue of mortgage taxation and finally gave up on it when friends in California advised him that a referendum there had shown its unpopularity with creditors and debtors alike. By 1904 or 1905 he became convinced that an income tax was the only politically effective way to reach invisible wealth.

As La Follette began to stress the voters' common interests as consumers and taxpayers, he paid increasingly little attention to the state's ethnic and religious groups. He hoped that Scandinavians would continue to support him because, as H. M. Thorvik wrote in 1904, "a good many Norwegians have received government positions." Evangelicals thanked him for banning illegal boxing matches, but they cursed him for not assisting local officials in enforcing state Sunday-closing laws. La Follette feared that he would lose support if he angered either side of the morals issue. To the extent that voters identified with their ethnic and religious backgrounds, they would not identify with the common consumer and taxpayer roles, as insurgency demanded.

In 1906, therefore, he clashed with his constituents over the issue of his successor as governor. Lieutenant Governor James Davidson, popular among the Norwegians, became acting governor early in 1906 when La Follette moved to the Senate, and he wanted to be renominated that year. La Follette, however, ordered his lieutenants to support Assembly Speaker Irvine Lenroot, a more committed insurgent who represented the far less numerous Swedes. "It would be inconsistent and unjust," La Follette wrote a friend who questioned the wisdom of opposing a popular Norwegian incumbent, "to allow nationality to be a determining factor with this wide difference [in ideologies]." His closest Norwegian lieutenants, Tax Commissioner Nils P. Haugen and Congressman John M. Nelson, bolted. "I am not going to be a fool and I am not going to be a traitor," exclaimed Nelson. La Follette snapped back that Nelson was committing "the error of self-assurance, over-confidence, and cock-suredness" by defying him. But La Follette was unable to win German support for Lenroot whose attitude toward liquor was nearly prohibitionist. The Norwegians and Germans rose up and rebuked La Follette. Davidson easily won the state's first direct primary, with 64 per cent of the vote, and he carried all but one county.

Lenroot's defeat in 1906 was the worst political humiliation of La Follette's career. He had not allowed his supporters to develop on their own into major spokesmen or leaders; and he believed so much in ideology that he cared less about the feelings of ethnic groups. He interpreted Lenroot's defeat, however, as a Norwegian failure, saying, "The people abused the opportunity which the primary election law offered. . . . I believed that long years of educational work in our campaigns had established higher standards of citizenship. . . . There is much work still to be done." La Follette forgot that the Scandinavians' lack of concern with issues was precisely what had allowed him to define issues without fear of voter contradiction. But in 1905 and 1906, as he was moving from Madison to Washington, La Follette was less interested in Wisconsin's ethnic blocs than in the national insurgent movement that many commentators expected him to lead.

Until 1903, La Follette, like most Americans, had little sense of a national movement. He sought help from Minnesota for the direct primary, Michigan for the railroad tax, Iowa and Texas for railroad regulation, and Massachusetts for civil service reform, and he knew in 1902 that his program was similar to those of Governors S. R. Van Sant in Minnesota and Albert Cummins in Iowa. But he saw nothing remarkable in the fact that Republican governors from neighboring states were promoting the same things.

About 1903 Americans began to believe that a new national movement was developing. The rapid evolution of new forms of mass, national communications bred the sense of unity between reformers in different communities. The rebirth of nationalism in the Spanish-American War, the phenomenal rise of new national monopolies and labor unions between 1897 and 1903, and the growing realization that other communities shared their problems led insurgent voters to create national agencies of communication that would speak to readers' uneasiness about the future, their consumer-taxpayer consciousness, and their fascination with scandal as the popular newspapers had done at the local level in the 1890s. The new national magazines and their muckraking journalists made readers in Toledo realize that St. Louis had the same problems and readers in St. Louis that Cleveland had found an answer. Muckrakers were trying to discover and explain the values that held people together amid widespread social unrest. They revealed in detail how events affected readers directly, and they were popular because, as Steffens said, they were only one step ahead of their readers' own experiences. The muckrakers maintained that individual reformers had singlehandedly changed things because readers wanted to believe that individuals could still control events, because readers shared vicariously the individual reformer's discovery of an evil, and because an account of individual action was more dramatic than complicated social analysis.

From 1903 to 1905 the muckrakers emphasized the common ground between La Follette and other reformers like Joseph Folk in Missouri or Ben Lindsey in Denver. "We like to think that our movement is part of the whole," a Toledo insurgent wrote La Follette after his city had installed an insurgent mayor. The muckrakers created the sense of a national movement by introducing its leaders to each other and to their readers. La Follette also found that he could rely on national popular magazines like *World's Work, Collier's, Saturday Evening Post,* and *McClure's* to expose his enemies. Nebraska's readers of La Follette's 1905 exposure and analysis of the railroad rate problem in the *Saturday Evening Post* were so impressed that they passed a stronger rate bill in their legislature than La Follette himself had secured in Wisconsin. La Follette became more comfortable and effective raising issues with muckrakers than he was with the politicians in his own legislature.

La Follette's major problem as a reform governor was not his lack of rapport with the legislature as a whole, however, but his inability to embrace completely the issues and methods of Wisconsin's insurgents. As a party leader, he could not understand why they wanted to give power directly to voters to make laws through the initiative and referendum process. He practiced representative, not direct, democracy. He had not seen the local utilities reach one reform official after another until desperation drove voters to demand the power to make laws without any politicians to intervene. Nor had he seen insurgent publicists directing popular pressure on city councils and thus share their faith that direct majority rule offered the best hope for the consumer and taxpayer.

La Follette's failures were not unique among statewide reform leaders. Only one insurgent overcame the greater barriers of timing, constitutional blocks, and partisanship at the state level and effectively translated the local pressures for direct popular rule to the state level. He was William S. U'Ren of Oregon. Shunning elective office, U'Ren steered through the statewide initiative and referendum in 1902, and he encouraged voters to mount petition campaigns so that they, not the legislature, would make policy. By 1912, Oregon's voters faced 37 issues on the ballot, deciding more important measures than the average state legislative session ever enacted. But Governor La Follette was not interested in the Oregon System.

La Follette also failed to understand why local insurgents wanted the power to deal with their enemies at the local level. As a state-level politician, he did not want to surrender any of the state's stranglehold over its cities, and local insurgents would not win home rule until 1924. He did not seem to understand that, from an insurgent point of view, the state level had constitutional, traditional, and structural drawbacks that made it much more responsive to ethnic, partisan, and job-oriented blocs than the local level and less responsive to consumer and taxpayer pressures.

La Follette's weaknesses, in the end, were those of many insurgent progressive governors, and they resulted from the middle ground those governors held between the old ethnic, job-oriented politics and the new issue-oriented politics. Insurgents often left their rear flanks exposed to ethnic counterattacks, as La Follette did in 1906, and they lacked the will and ability to become the shrewd parliamentary manipulators that old-style politicians had been. By not moving far enough toward the issue politics, they were victims of the baggage they still carried from the old politics. By viewing their elections as the basic reform and not mobilizing public opinion toward legislation, they failed to unleash the real power that existed within insurgency. For these reasons insurgent governors like La Follette failed to secure the truly radical laws that would have transformed American society in the ways implied in their rhetoric. The Senate freed them from these administrative and factional problems, and many of them soon gladly followed La Follette to Washington.

I V

The Development
of National Insurgency
1906–1910

THE GALLERIES were hushed as the Senate came to
order on January 4, 1906. Custom called for Senator John Coit
Spooner, brilliant spokesman for the old politics, to present
his new junior colleague from Wisconsin, La Follette. Everyone knew that Spooner and La Follette exemplified the two
ideologies and styles that were struggling for control of the
Republican Party. Spooner rose. Would he challenge La Follette's title? Spooner presented La Follette's credentials, walked
to the rear of the Senate, offered La Follette his right arm,
and escorted him up the center aisle to receive the oath. "An
audible sigh swept down from the galleries as the tension relaxed," recalled La Follette. That night, at a White House
diplomatic reception, Senator and Mrs. La Follette again felt
that official Washington was looking them over, trying to decide
whether La Follette was going to revolutionize their political
world. "I think if I had been a wild boar, led about by Mrs. La
Follette with a rope fastened to my hind leg, as a pair, we
would not have been more observed," La Follette wrote friends.

La Follette's arrival in Washington coincided with accelerating popular protests not just in Wisconsin but throughout
the country. He would soon be joined by insurgent senators

from other states. But in 1906, as La Follette arrived, most voters looked to President Theodore Roosevelt for reform leadership in Washington. Although Roosevelt would later condemn insurgent politicians and muckrakers as dangerous radicals, he was responsive enough to public opinion to be "the first political leader . . . to identify the national principle with the ideal of reform," as journalist Herbert Croly wrote. Roosevelt used the presidency as a "bully pulpit" from which to denounce "wrongdoers" who widened the gap between rich and poor. His instinctive rapport with newsmen established his reputation as a reformer, and his impetuous temperament led him to innovate executive powers in such areas of insurgent concern as corporate regulation, labor relations, and conservation.

It was Congress that most concerned La Follette, for the rapid growth of large corporations in the late nineteenth and early twentieth centuries had produced a politics designed to protect and advance corporate interests. In the Senate, Republican leaders such as Nelson W. Aldrich of Rhode Island believed that the new corporations had destroyed the traditional basis of politics in which legislators represented voters from isolated geographic units, a politics that had emphasized sectional hatreds between North and South, East and West. Aldrich, Spooner, and other Senate leaders used the Republican caucus to mobilize the party's Senate majority behind the needs of economic interests instead of sectional ones. The caucus would listen to the legislative proposals of corporations, formulate a bill, and then use all the instruments of senatorial discipline — committee assignments, campaign funds, and patronage — to compel all Republican senators to support it. Party loyalty was a cardinal virtue, and the party should reward the corporations that financed its elections.

The Senate bosses, deeply threatened by the rapid growth of insurgency, viewed politicians like La Follette as demagogues, and muckrakers and yellow journalists like Steffens and William Randolph Hearst as scandalmongers who appealed to the depraved appetites and instinctive prejudices of the ignorant masses. They decided to sidetrack the hated La Follette as soon as he arrived by depriving him of any influence over important bills, so they made him chairman of the Committee to Investigate the Condition of the Potomac River Front, a committee that had never met, and buried him under a mass of routine business by appointing him to evaluate claims and pensions.

La Follette was not troubled by these appointments because he viewed the Senate as a forum from which to develop national issues for a future, less conservative, Senate to act on. He wanted to expose corporate domination over that body and to secure the future election of more insurgents. It was his great good luck that in 1906 muckrakers picked up the decade-old radical charge that the Senate, dominated by millionaires and corporations, was the leading obstruction to national insurgency.

In 1905 five Senators had been either convicted of defrauding the federal government or implicated in insurance scandals. Hearst, whose daily newspapers had promoted direct election of senators since 1899, turned his magazine, *Cosmopolitan,* to the cause in 1906. It published David Graham Phillips' nine-month series "Treason of the Senate," whose bold language and graphic detail appealed to readers' common interests as consumers, taxpayers, and citizens; to their common fascination with gossip, scandal, and combat; and to their common emotions of anger and fear. Phillips painted senators as "the eager, resourceful, indefatigable agents of interests as hostile to the American people as any invading army could be." In their spineless subservience to the "interests," Phillips charged, senators were reducing most Americans to "dependence" on the powerful. They lacked the courage, exemplified by La Follette and Roosevelt, to resist the powerful corporations. Americans could regain control over their lives, said Phillips, by sending new insurgents to join La Follette and demanding direct election of senators by the voters so that corporations could no longer dominate the state legislators who sent the traitors to Washington.

Sensing the voters' anger as consumers and taxpayers, La Follette set out to show how insurgency transformed older issues to accommodate the voters' anger and how Congress could provide solutions. As he tried to make issues more responsive to consumer consciousness, La Follette incorporated his personal need to establish a record with the insurgents' political need to expose the dependence of senators upon favored corporations. Thus, as a member of the innocuous Indian Affairs Committee, he turned a routine bill for Oklahoma's Five Civilized Tribes into a major issue to the millions of Americans who stayed warm in winter by burning coal. Exposing a provision that allowed the railroads to buy the huge coal reserves on the Indian lands, he showed how monopolistic ownership of coal supplies by railroads would mean higher prices to coal consumers. As journalists and voters applauded his stand, he introduced a resolution on June 20, 1906, "in the interest of the coal and oil consumers," that authorized the president to withdraw from sale all public mineral lands until Congress could guarantee competition and hence lower prices. He did not care that the Senate ignored the resolution for, as he wrote Belle, "It will be one of the *great questions*."

La Follette established an independent stance as the consumer's champion during debate on the most important law of 1906, the Hepburn Act regulating railroads. President Roosevelt promoted the Hepburn Act so that organized shippers could appeal to the Interstate Commerce Commission to modify rail rates that discriminated against them. La Follette, on the other hand, wanted a law that would benefit "the helpless consumer," and he grew convinced that the Hepburn Act would benefit only shippers. He planned a dramatic appeal. La Follette never expected senators to support his position (for Roosevelt was having trouble with even his moderate bill), but he planned to put all senators on record with public roll calls on his amendments. He would then expose those senators who had voted against his amendments as enemies that consumers must defeat.

On April 19, 1906, he violated the Senate's unwritten rule against speeches by freshmen with a speech that lasted several days and ran to 148 printed pages. As La Follette started to speak, senators closed their books and newspapers and walked off the floor, leaving La Follette alone with the crowded galleries. La Follette lashed back, warning that the insurgent majority of consumers suspected senators of treason, and the senators were convicting themselves by walking out. "Senators by their absence at this time indicate their want of interest in what I may have to say upon this subject. The public is interested. Unless this important question is rightly settled seats now temporarily vacant may be permanently vacated by those who have the right to occupy them at this time." Belle, sitting in the galleries, was stunned by her husband's challenge, but felt relieved when the galleries broke into applause. He was, after all, appealing to the galleries.

La Follette declared that "the welfare of all the people as consumers should be the supreme consideration of the Government," and charged that the Hepburn bill ignored the ultimate consumer who paid railroad rates in the form of higher prices. Consumers were ignored because they were too unorganized. "The whole history of this struggle . . . reveals the fact that those who are strong through the power of organization and wealth fare the best," he said. The organized rich received special privileges from government that defied "the natural law of trade and commerce." Property acquired by special privilege was robbery, and "the thief can have no vested rights in stolen property." The battle to reassert community discipline was "the highest patriotism" and might ultimately require the government to own the railroads. La Follette's consumer-oriented insurgency thus drew upon two previously antagonistic ethics: the youthful capitalists' love of competition and the preindustrial culture's love of community.

La Follette's most important amendment reflected his interest in giving power to the consumer. It gave the ICC the power to initiate complaints without awaiting shipper protests and empowered it to make rates on the basis of the railroads' physical property. The Senate rejected it 40 to 27 with his other amendments, including one prohibiting judges from hearing ICC appeals if they owned stock in the railroad involved in the case. But the muckrakers and daily press praised his battle for the consumer. Belle reported that newspaper correspondents "know that something has happened, and the Senate knows that something has happened, and that there is a new power they cannot down."

When the Senate adjourned at the end of June, La Follette sought vindication for the rejection of his amendments in a five-month speaking campaign in the West. He needed money to pay for the $30,000 farm he and Belle had bought near Madison in the fall of 1905, for Fola's training to become an actress, and for the younger children's private schools. He compared himself to the tattletaling child who won approval by reporting others' misdeeds. Senators, he told Belle, would probably "think I am the meanest fellow ever to 'go and tell.' " La Follette's personal need for a record coincided perfectly with insurgency's emphasis on exposure and with voters' suspicions after they had read the latest "Treason of the Senate" installment.

La Follette appealed to voters' vague uneasiness over the country's social development. Like the muckrakers, he described his discovery that large privileged corporations were simultaneously destroying the ethics of competition and community. His listeners shared his sense of discovery. "This emotion which you aroused in me," wrote Abraham Deixel of Newark after hearing La Follette, "is the same as that which originally prompted you to spur on to the fighting line." La Follette was effective precisely because voters were already disturbed, for, as he wrote Belle, "the . . . people . . . are in the midst of experiences which make them ready for the gos-

pel." After describing his campaign to amend the Hepburn
Act, he read the roll call on his amendments as nervous
audiences awaited their senator's name. He read the roll in
sixteen states in 1906. H. B. Walker of the *Newark News*
reported that "the whole success or failure of the movement
may depend, and to my mind does largely depend upon you,"
as La Follette gave sixteen speeches in six days in New Jersey.

Although La Follette had used the roll call earlier in Wisconsin, most national journalists and politicians were stunned
by the dramatic effect it was having. By late November the
New York Times reported that "the devastation created by La
Follette last summer and in the early fall was much greater
than had been supposed. He carried senatorial discourtesy so
far that he has actually imperiled the reelection of some of the
gentlemen who hazed him last winter." Rejecting party discipline, lobbyists, and senatorial courtesy, La Follette established his insurgent leadership by making this ultimate use of
the insurgent weapon of exposure.

La Follette paid a high personal price for these Chautauqua
speeches. Local groups wanted to talk with him, and he could
not adequately prepare. He would toss at night after a poor
speech. Trains would run late, and he would miss scheduled
dates and the income from them. To reach Waterville, he took
a train to the Columbia River landing, a steamboat for twenty
miles, and then a four-hour stagecoach ride. It was a grueling,
hot, lonely, sleepless grind punctuated by constant guilt over
the long separations from his family. "If we can hold on for
another year," he wrote Belle, "and I can make a full season
next summer then we will be out of debt and take things easy
and have life together." Nine-year-old Phil replied simply: "I
want you more at home with us than you are."

When La Follette returned to the "dear old rotten Senate"
in early December, he learned from journalists that the Senate
bosses were searching for ways to discipline him. "The air is
surcharged," he wrote Belle, "due to the fact that I continue

to hear that the subject of 'What we ought to do with La Follette' . . . is still under consideration by the men who think they are responsible for the Senate."

La Follette won his first battle. He promoted a bill to prohibit railroad workers from working more than sixteen consecutive hours. He reported to Belle that "the fear of the roll call which has entered men's souls was very noticeable yesterday" when the Senate adopted his bill in January by a 36-to-32 vote and thirteen Republicans bolted their leaders to vote with him. The *New York Times* observed that La Follette's roll call campaign was responsible for the bill's passage, and the *Washington Times* called it "a triumph of the Record."

The 1907 Railway Hours Act revealed how insurgency's consumer consciousness developed its prolabor orientation. H. R. Fuller, the railroad brotherhoods' lobbyist, had realized that La Follette's hatred of railroad managers would make him support the brotherhoods' measures. He had persuaded La Follette to introduce the sixteen-hour-bill in 1906, but Congress had not acted then. In the intervening months journalists had graphically illustrated La Follette's argument that the bill was necessary to reduce the deaths and injuries to passengers in railroad wrecks: in a single year 10,617 passengers and 48,487 railway workers had been killed or injured in wrecks. The muckrakers and La Follette attributed the wrecks to overworked employees. The best way to protect consumers when they were railroad passengers, said La Follette, was to ensure workers enough rest.

The 1907 debate was more consumer-oriented than that of 1906 because conservative senators produced opposition from hundreds of railway employees. La Follette charged that railway officials had extorted signatures by threatening to fire workers who did not sign. When some workers complained that the bill deprived them of overtime pay, La Follette replied that the need of the travelling public for safety was more important than the greed of either railway officials or workers.

By linking the haunting fear of death in a wreck to the cause of consumers, La Follette secured the law for the brotherhoods and found, as Belle reported from Madison, "a measure that seized hold of the popular mind."

In early 1907 La Follette appealed to consumers in another area — conservation — and he expected support from Roosevelt as he took on the Senate bosses. Behind the debate were conflicting attitudes toward natural resources. Western conservative Republicans favored immediate exploitation and wanted no restrictions on grazing, mining, or power development, insisting that their region was entitled to the same unimpeded resource exploitation that had produced economic growth in more settled areas. Roosevelt wanted to give trained experts like Chief Forester Gifford Pinchot broad discretionary powers to administer resource lands in order to guarantee a future supply of resources while producing stable economic growth. He viewed conservation largely as a problem of production, planning, and economic growth. La Follette, on the other hand, mainly wanted to protect consumers from the high prices that would result from monopolistic ownership of the lands. Besides championing competition, La Follette wanted to hold individual businessmen responsible for any misuse of public lands and, unlike Roosevelt, favored fining and imprisoning offenders. Both Roosevelt and La Follette agreed that the immediate solution was for the government to hold title to the mineral lands and to preserve control by leasing them.

Early in the session Roosevelt had promised to support La Follette's bill to withdraw mineral lands from corporate exploitation; and La Follette felt betrayed when the president, alarmed by the protest that greeted La Follette's introduction of the bill, backed down and supported a weaker bill. The uneasy relationship between La Follette and Roosevelt deteriorated further in mid-February when the president withdrew his promised support of physical valuation of railroad properties by the ICC. When La Follette complained bitterly to Belle that Roosevelt "throws me down every day or so," Belle reminded him that "everyone . . . is pleased with the idea that *you are working with the President.* This is what the public is prepared to expect and eager to believe." La Follette therefore kept his bitterness to himself and enjoyed widespread speculation that he was Roosevelt's logical successor since they were both part of the same movement.

When the short session adjourned in March 1907, La Follette took again to the Chautauqua circuit, speaking in seventeen states in 1907, thirteen of them west of the Mississippi. Local committees sympathetic to conservative Republican incumbents tried to stop him from reading the roll at Pittsburgh and Walla Walla, Washington, but with no luck. The *Seattle Star* took up La Follette's attack on Washington Senator Levi Ankeney. The high point of his tour came at San Francisco, where he became friendly with local insurgents who were prosecuting the city's business elite for graft.

La Follette was sometimes alarmed by his supporters. He complained that businessmen in Montana favored his plan for railroad regulation not "from patriotic motives," but because "they are too eager for wealth and rate it too high." After listening to speeches extolling the wealth of nearby mines at a Montana Club banquet in his honor at Helena, he waited until 1:30 A.M. to tell the audience "that they had interested and amazed me with their marvelous production of copper, but I'd like to know what kind of men they were producing — what kind of citizenship they were building into their new commonwealth."

La Follette could not see that behind the temporary unity of consumers, taxpayers, and citizens there lay a basic conflict between the two values he espoused: competition and community. Competition had fostered the very materialist values in the Montana businessmen that he deplored, but he still believed that competition offered the best way for the united community of consumers to discipline the new industrial corporations. He would continue to receive support from those who yearned for a restoration of competition and of community so long as voters were united as consumers.

The success of La Follette's roll call campaign ironically created a problem which showed that he was still a factional politician as well as an insurgent. Early in 1907 John Coit Spooner announced that he would not run for reelection to the Senate in 1908. "The deadly roll call deterred him," La Follette believed. "He shrank from the review of his record which he knew was coming . . . to have a whole campaign on that record, his votes read and jibed and slurred and innuendoed and openly charged and plain proven to be a betrayal of his state and country." His resignation forced the Wisconsin legislature, controlled by La Follette's friends, to elect a successor. Lumber baron Isaac Stephenson, the financial angel for the La Follette organization, demanded the job. Many of La Follette's lieutenants balked, insisting that the state be represented by a committed insurgent like Irvine Lenroot. For seven weeks the legislature was unable to decide. Finally, La Follette sent the order: "Stephenson must win. Fight hard." Stephenson did win, but the decision split La Follette's organization less than a year after it had divided over his insistence on nominating a committed insurgent over a popular Norwegian for governor. By supporting Stephenson, as Belle reminded him, he seemed to have surrendered principle to money.

During the Senate session that met from late 1907 until mid-1908 La Follette located what he would believe for the rest of his life was the major source of the country's economic and political problems. The financial Panic of 1907 provided the setting for Nelson Aldrich's proposal to issue $500 million in emergency currency backed by state, municipal, and railroad bonds. As La Follette resisted the bill to support public currency with private railroad bonds, he broadened his insurgent analysis.

The fundamental problem with the economy, charged La Follette, was that fewer than 100 businessmen affiliated with the Standard Oil and Morgan investment banking houses "dominate and control the business and industrial life of this country." Serving as directors of the largest industrial and transportation companies, these investment bankers, whom he called the Money Trust, could abolish competition in an industry, establish labor policies, ignore consumers, and even alter the business cycle at will. Few politicians dared attack them because of their economic power.

La Follette documented his case in March 1908 with earlier muckraking exposures and with the names of the corporations directed by the 97 members of the Money Trust, a list that filled twelve pages in the *Congressional Record*. The Money Trust, La Follette charged, had artificially created and manipulated the Panic of 1907 to drive out its competitors and compel the government to restore investor confidence in railroad securities by using them, as Aldrich planned, as backing for emergency currency. The Money Trust also created the Panic to destroy insurgency by seeming to show that the insurgents' new regulations on business produced depressions. Since the Money Trust controlled the utilities and railroads insurgents were fighting in their cities and states, consumers could not secure relief until the bankers, interested only in the profits on securities, were forced to surrender their industrial holdings.

As La Follette discovered the insurgents' ultimate villain, he contrasted the insurgents' social vision with that of the Money Trust. To insurgents, "home, children, neighbors, friends, church, schools, country constitute life." People did not want artificial economic distinctions to change the familiar pattern of "conscience and human emotion" in their daily lives. The Money Trust, however, envisioned such complete economic concentration that it could readily destroy familiar community habits. Behind the investment bankers, said La Follette, "is the THING which we must destroy if we would preserve our free institutions. Men are as nothing; the System which we have built up by privileges, which we have allowed to take possession of Government and control legislation" must be destroyed. The System must be prevented from enshrining concentrated units of economic power as the basis of society.

La Follette agreed with insurgent sociologist Edward A. Ross that in order to discipline the large corporation, the community must be able to fix responsibility on evil individuals. Ross had argued in *Sin and Society* (1907) that Americans should learn that corporate arrogance was criminal and sinful, that "boodling is treason, that blackmail is piracy, that embezzlement is theft, that speculation is gambling, that tax-dodging is larceny, that railroad discrimination is treachery, that factory labor of children is slavery, that deleterious adulteration is murder." The corporation "transmits the greed of investors, but not their conscience; that returns them profits, but not unpopularity." In the spirit of fixing personal responsibility, La Follette secured an amendment to the 1908 currency act that made it a crime for bankers to submit lies in their reports to the government.

La Follette decided to dramatize his opposition to the Money Trust by trying to filibuster to death the Aldrich-Vreeland currency bill. Aldrich tried to compel this bill's passage by withholding until the last minute a bill with provisions for public buildings in most states. Assured of support from Democrats William Stone of Missouri and Thomas Gore of Oklahoma, La Follette began his filibuster at noon on May 29, 1908, the day before adjournment. He had no idea how long he could last since he was fighting a cold.

With the temperature over 90 degrees on the Senate floor, La Follette ramblingly attacked the bill and Aldrich's dictatorial control over legislation. Tempers ran short. Senators and congressmen talked noisily. La Follette tried to humiliate conservatives by announcing when one was absent, glaring at another, or asking a third to stop using sign language. He saved his strength by demanding quorum calls — more than thirty — which consumed six or seven minutes each. By midnight he had consumed two turkey sandwiches and six glasses of milk and eggs. At one point he took a gulp from a glass of milk and eggs from the Senate restaurant and cried: "Take it away; it's drugged." (Subsequent chemical analysis revealed that it had contained enough ptomaine to have killed him if he had drunk the whole glass.) La Follette finally yielded the floor to Stone at 7:05 the next morning. His nineteen-hour filibuster was a new Senate record. Stone gave way to Gore at 2:00 P.M. and, after speaking two hours, the blind Gore, assuming that Stone was present, yielded the floor. Stone was not there. Vice-President Charles W. Fairbanks quickly recognized Aldrich, and the bill passed 43 to 22.

During his attack on the Money Trust, La Follette had prophesied that Wall Street control of the nation's economy and politics was so complete that manufacturers "made desperate by oppression [will] join at last with the consumers of the country in open revolt." The Wilmington (Delaware) Board of Trade and Boston Chamber of Commerce opposed the Aldrich-Vreeland Act. The New York Board of Trade asked for twenty-five copies of La Follette's speech to circulate among its most active members. His office was deluged by requests for the Money Power speech, and, more important, the pattern of those requests was different from that for requests of his earlier Senate speeches: the Midwest had generated 85 per cent of the requests for his earlier speeches, but the Eastern metropolitan corridor provided almost half of the requests for the Money Power speech. A Philadelphia businessman telegraphed La Follette after the filibuster: "The Commercial Interests of the country are profoundly interested in your magnificent and heroic fight. This Memorial Day commemorates no braver act of public duty." Conservative newspapers might decry La Follette's blast at the Money Trust as the paranoid rantings of a populistic Westerner, but a great many businessmen praised it as a remarkably accurate analysis.

By insisting that cities and states could achieve only minor gains until Congress dismantled the Money Trust, La Follette contributed to the growing feeling among many insurgents that national solutions were the only permanent ones possible for the local and immediate problems that had originally sparked insurgency. La Follette knew that national focus inevitably meant a campaign for an insurgent president. Muckraking magazines exposed fewer local abuses in late 1907 and 1908 and talked more about presidential candidates. Steffens explained in *Everybody's Magazine* in 1908 that La Follette was the logical successor to Theodore Roosevelt because he understood how "The System" controlled politics and business. Hearst, whose newspapers had championed local campaigns for municipal ownership, tax reform, and direct democracy, believed by 1908 that the only solution would be to elect an insurgent president. He formed the Independence League in 1908 and tried unsuccessfully to persuade La Follette to be the candidate.

La Follette hoped that these pressures would commit the national Republican Party to his leadership. On October 29, 1907, his Wisconsin lieutenants had launched the La Follette-for-President campaign, and, to reassure unhappy Norwegians, he named Assembly Speaker Herman Ekern to direct it. La Follette linked his candidacy to a declaration of principles he wanted the party platform to contain — mostly issues he had earlier raised, particularly physical valuation of railroads. He argued that Wisconsin under his governorship had pioneered in adopting insurgent programs and that he was, therefore, the most logical candidate to advance national insurgency. "The present of Wisconsin is the future of America," wrote his friend John R. Commons in the *North American Review*.

La Follette's campaign suffered from his insistence on entrusting it to his Wisconsin lieutenants. Ekern and the lieutenants gathered names of former Wisconsinites living in other states, and these expatriated Badgers managed the La Follette campaigns in their states. The Wisconsin men had no previous national experience or exposure; the *Washington Post* continually misspelled Ekern's name. La Follette had complained in 1906 to New Jersey's insurgent State Senator Everett Colby that his Wisconsin organization lacked the brains and vision of Colby's New Jersey colleagues ("It is so hard to make bricks without straw"), but in his own presidential campaign La Follette asked only for complete loyalty — and that he received from his lieutenants. But in the end his aides were only able to secure delegates from the state where they had experience — Wisconsin. Although delegates from seventeen states supported at least one of his proposed planks, his platform was overwhelmingly defeated and he won only the votes of Wisconsin delegates for his presidential bid. Even so, La Follette was pleased that the platform promised to revise the tariff and that candidate William Howard Taft sounded as though he wanted to continue Roosevelt's policies.

Many commentators believed that La Follette's real contribution in 1908 was his influence in changing the composition of the Senate. They credited La Follette with the 1908 victories of insurgent Republicans Joseph L. Bristow in Kansas, Coe I. Crawford in South Dakota, Albert Cummins in Iowa, and the defeat of reactionary Senator John F. Dryden in New Jersey. "Old-Timers at the Capitol say the like of La Follette's crusade against his colleagues has never before been known in the history of the Senate," observed the *Washington National Tribune*: "No one can forecast the possibilities of this growing progressive force." Although La Follette did indeed contribute to this "force" by campaigning for insurgent challengers to conservative senators, he was effective precisely because other communities were experiencing grassroots revolts similar to the ones that had led to his victories in Wisconsin.

As La Follette waited for the Senate to convene in 1909, he launched a new venture that combined his zeal for the insurgent cause with his eagerness for financial security, as his Chautauqua lectures had. Since he had sold his college newspaper thirty years earlier, he wanted another journal to spread the gospel. Although Belle warned that it might prevent the family from achieving financial security, La Follette insisted that he would make a "couple of fortunes" from it.

He launched *La Follette's Weekly Magazine* on January 9, 1909. La Follette was the editor, Belle ran the "Home and Education" department, and his children wrote articles whenever they wanted. The Roll Call became a prominent feature; it listed votes on measures that interested La Follette and exposed the entire records of particular senators and congressmen who opposed his positions. La Follette also used the magazine for his personal needs. He ran free advertisements for the Mitchell-Lewis Car Company when the company gave him a free car in 1911. The magazine's circulation ranged between 30,000 and 48,000 in its early years, with about half in Wisconsin. Although La Follette's lieutenants hustled subscriptions, the magazine had a precarious financial existence from the start. La Follette counted on large contributions from wealthy insurgents like bathtub magnate Charles Crane, Wall Street financier E. Clarence Jones, and Rudolph Spreckels to keep it alive.

"Ye Shall Know the Truth and the Truth Shall Make You Free" was emblazoned on the magazine's masthead, and it reflected La Follette's and the insurgent public's faith that corporate and political corruption would cease once exposed and publicized. The magazine's inspirational stories about insurgent victories in cities and states hinged on a strong man or woman discovering evil and campaigning to persuade others of the discovery. For example, James A. Peterson had "singlehandedly" elected an insurgent city council in Minneapolis by publishing roll calls that revealed the incumbents' subservience to the utilities.

La Follette's reflected the muckrakers' growing private conviction by 1909 or 1910 that their earlier exposures had not struck deeply enough at fundamental evils, their growing belief that the current need was less for exposures than for specific programs to change The System. The magazine promoted commission and manager forms of city governments as near-panaceas for the problems of municipal corruption. By substituting structure for spirit, leaders for voters, and The System for immediate grievances, insurgents may have abandoned their initial faith that unorganized mass arousal could sustain their movement and produce permanently effective changes.

The La Follettes' new home on Washington's fashionable northwest side provided a congenial atmosphere for the Senate insurgents to plan their strategies in the special Congressional session that Taft called in 1909 to fulfill the party's pledge to revise the tariff. As it became clearer that Aldrich had no intention of lowering the tariff, the insurgents began to cooperate so closely that they seemed to be a new party caucus. La Follette was their leader, but he believed that Jonathan P. Dolliver of Iowa was their heart. For years the gregarious Dolliver had supported the Senate bosses; he had worshipped his senior Iowa colleague William B. Allison, a Senate leader. When Allison died in 1908 and Aldrich refused Dolliver a coveted position, Dolliver, following his natural instincts and his constituents' desires, joined the insurgents. He brought his good friend, the relaxed, tolerant Moses Clapp of Minnesota, to the insurgents. Beveridge of Indiana, youngest of the group, had been converted by the muckrakers, particularly his close friend David Graham Phillips. Flashy, egotistical, brilliant, Beveridge loved debate and relentlessly prosecuted Aldrich. The dignified, scholarly, humorless Albert Cummins of Iowa was one of the newcomers in 1909, but he had demanded lower tariff duties to protect consumers longer than any of them. The hardest worker among the insurgents was also a newcomer, earnest Joseph Bristow of Kansas, who bristled with moral outrage. On particular issues the movement also included Knute Nelson of Minnesota, Coe Crawford of South Dakota, Norris Brown and Elmer Burkett of Nebraska, William Borah of Idaho, and Jonathan Bourne of Oregon.

The insurgent cause was so important to them that all bases

of difference — different ethno-religious backgrounds and the customary jealousies between senators — evaporated. Fanatical prohibitionist Bristow never complained when Dolliver or Clapp drank during their nightly strategy meetings at the Beveridges' apartment or the La Follettes' home. As the sultry Washington summer approached and as the cumulative effect of four or five hours' sleep a night produced shortened tempers, the insurgents appreciated old Moses Clapp. Clapp listened to his colleagues while he quietly drank bottle after bottle of beer, and then he proposed the solution they usually adopted. They all felt, as Belle wrote about her husband, "glad, deeply glad, of the fellowship, companionship, and understanding" they provided each other. Beveridge contrasted to his wife his days as a lieutenant in the Aldrich Senate machine when he had been "a cipher — a nought in a servile bunch of men" with his days among his zealous, independent insurgent colleagues. They never doubted their course because they believed that they represented their party's official position in its 1908 platform and the majority of aroused consumers.

The voices of these consumers came from many directions. Residents of Wisconsin, Illinois, and Massachusetts petitioned Congress for lower duties on the "necessaries of life." Middle-class clubwomen mounted the most obvious campaign in such cities as Detroit, Denver, and Chicago. By April 3, 1909, the Chicago clubwomen had 100,000 signatures on a petition demanding lower duties on the "absolute necessities of feminine life." But the protest came from all classes. The *Washington Post* lumped ditchdiggers with clergymen as part of the "mighty army of consumers" demanding relief. Protective duties placed "a heavier burden on the weary backs of the poor," explained the *New York Times,* because they lacked the organization of wealthy lobbyists. During the debate, insurgents identified their consumers: poor workers and farmers for Bristow, "humble homes" for Cummins, and workers existing at the poverty line for Beveridge.

For the first time in two generations Americans were experiencing desperate inflation in which prices rose faster than incomes. From 1865 to 1897 workers had gained from a general deflationary trend: wages had fallen less than 10 per cent while prices in general had fallen 35 to 40 per cent and prices of necessities had fallen even more sharply — food by 61 per cent, fuel by 70 per cent. Workers were thus unprepared for the dramatic onset of inflation in 1897. From 1897 to 1909, wages rose about 22 per cent while prices in general rose about 35 per cent and prices on necessities rose even faster — food by 37 per cent, fuel by 53 per cent. Angered and frustrated by this new inflationary experience, consumer-oriented Americans came to believe that the basic cause of soaring prices was the sudden growth of trusts and monopolies, which raised their prices as they curtailed their competition. In the six years before 1897, 42 important "trusts" were formed, but in the next six years, 317 important trusts began, including such giants as U.S. Steel, International Harvester, and Standard Oil. The total capitalization of all million-dollar corporations skyrocketed 120 times from 1897 to 1904, from $170 million to $20 billion. The cause of the rapid growth of monopolies was also obvious: the Republican-sponsored Dingley Tariff of 1897 that had raised duties so high that American manufacturers could combine and charge higher prices without fear of foreign competition. Blue-collar and white-collar workers felt equally threatened, and they united as consumers. "We hear a great deal about the class-consciousness of labor," observed Walter Lippmann. "My own observation is that in America today consumers' consciousness is growing very much faster." Other analysts agreed with Lippmann. "The unifying economic force, about which a majority, hostile to the plutocracy, is forming," noted Walter Weyl, "is the common interest of the citizen as a consumer of wealth. . . . Men who voted as producers are now voting as consumers."

Aldrich and the Republican leaders proceeded to draft the Payne-Aldrich Tariff as though the consumer protest did not exist. As in the past, the Republican members of the Finance Committee wrote the bill to fit the requests of job-oriented interest groups and particularly corporation managers. They echoed hallowed Republican doctrines from the nineteenth century: protection encouraged infant industries to develop and protected the jobs of American workers from cheaper foreign competition. When they enacted lower duties it was to give manufacturers cheaper raw materials, not to help consumers. Prosperity, a basic goal for Aldrich, was created by manufacturers and workers, and they needed a high tariff to preserve it. Aldrich and the conservatives denied the existence of consumer protest. "Who are the consumers in the United States?" asked Aldrich. Henry Cabot Lodge of Massachusetts attacked the insurgents' "myth of a consuming public." "Where is this separate and isolated public of consumers? . . . This is a Nation of producers." Charles W. F. Dick of Ohio underscored the conservatives' insistence on serving only well-organized pressure groups when he explained that consumers were not unhappy because "I have no communication from them."

La Follette and the insurgents insisted that the consumer protest against the Payne-Aldrich Tariff necessitated basic changes in old issues. By 1909 La Follette believed that the American consumer "raised such a storm" because the high duties were reaching "everything that goes upon his table, everything that goes to clothe and warm his family and provide for their comfort." Instead of fostering opportunity and encouraging infant industries, as he had expected in the 1880s, protection had only strengthened the monopolies. The *New York World* described La Follette's attack on the protectionist cotton duties as a "brief for the American housewife." "Greed tempered by absolute control," charged La Follette, "has advanced prices until the cost of living to the consumer . . . has been increased nearly 50 per cent." La Follette thus insisted that the tariff, one of the oldest issues in American politics, should respond no longer to producers' needs, but to the new direction of public opinion.

The consumer protest led insurgents to modify other nineteenth-century concepts as well. In the 1880s, Republicans like

Congressman La Follette had opposed monopoly on the basis of the producer-oriented argument that competition created opportunity and economic growth. In 1909, La Follette and other insurgents continued to favor competition because it created opportunity, but they now emphasized its role in providing consumers with the means to discipline producers. They no longer even mentioned economic growth. The absence of foreign competition meant not only that American manufacturers were combining and raising prices, but also that they were making inferior and increasingly unsafe products. Worse still, as Beveridge showed for the cash register trust, American manufacturers sold the same models in England for half the tariff-protected American price. "The right of the consumer of any article or commodity to competition is dearer and higher and more sacred than the right of the producer to protection," cried Cummins. The victim of monopoly was no longer the aspiring businessman or the country's economic growth, but the consumer.

Since tariff revenues constituted about one-half of federal revenues in 1908, any debate on the Payne-Aldrich Tariff was inevitably a debate over taxation. Taft wanted to compensate for lost tariff revenues by enacting a corporation tax. La Follette and the insurgents argued that the tariff was itself a tax on consumers and that corporations would only pass their taxes to the consumer. Viewing taxation as a means of redistributing wealth, insurgents argued that the tax burden should be shifted from poor consumers to rich producers and that a steeply graduated income tax was the best way to narrow the gulf between rich and poor. In the end, Taft applied enough pressure on wavering Republican senators to secure the corporation tax, but insurgent Republicans won enough Democratic votes to start the machinery for a constitutional amendment permitting an income tax.

The insurgents challenged Aldrich's and Taft's conception of a politician's obligation to his party and his constituents. Aldrich argued that the insurgent Republicans would be defeated for reelection because they had defied their party leaders; Taft cut off federal patronage to the insurgents. La Follette and the insurgents replied that the party platform bound a politician to his constituents and that they were trying to fulfill the GOP platform whereas Aldrich was subverting it. La Follette further charged that Aldrich had no conception of representative government because he came from the corrupt state of Rhode Island where the majority of voters were effectively disenfranchised. Dolliver warned, "The Republican Party is face to face, as in the days of its youth, with the elementary questions which concern justice and liberty."

The insurgents' four-month battle against the Payne-Aldrich Tariff in mid-1909 failed when the Senate passed it 47 to 31 on August 8, with La Follette, Beveridge, Bristow, Clapp, Cummins, Dolliver, and Nelson casting the only negative Republican votes. As the insurgents returned to their homes, they found overwhelming popular support for their position – even though it had divided the party. Cummins wrote Beveridge that his reception in Iowa was "a wonder" that proved "a deep and pervading belief that we have stood for the right things." Taft was stung deeply by the insurgents' charge that he was a mere pawn in Aldrich's hands. In September he made a month-long speaking tour of the Midwest in which he read the insurgents out of the party and defended "the best tariff bill" ever passed. Beveridge, who had never seen public opinion so united as it was now in support of the insurgents, was appalled by Taft's political stupidity. La Follette replied simply: "No individual has the power to read a representative out of his party. That power rests solely with the voters who selected him as their party representative." The party platform, La Follette insisted, was "an obligation higher than the mere demands of party solidarity under a misrepresentative leadership in Congress."

As La Follette made another roll call swing through the Far West in late 1909, he revealed anew the insurgents' faith that the power for change came from outside established political institutions, from exposure of wrongdoing by public roll calls or muckraking articles. The cooperation between muckrakers and insurgent politicians climaxed during the session that met from late 1909 until mid-1910, and it converted a quarrel among three bureaucrats into a popular crusade that seriously damaged President Taft and further divided the party. Louis Glavis, a minor figure in the Interior Department, became convinced that Taft's Interior Secretary, Richard A. Ballinger, was trying to hasten approval for the Morgan-Guggenheim interests to acquire rich Alaskan coal lands, an illegal violation of the Roosevelt conservation crusade. Encouraged by Chief Forester Gifford Pinchot, one of Roosevelt's closest friends, Glavis's took his story to Taft. But instead of sympathy, as Pinchot and Glavis had expected, Taft supported his Interior Secretary and promptly ordered Glavis fired for insubordination.

Glavis told the muckrakers, and the November 1909 issue of *Collier's Weekly* carried Glavis's charge that Ballinger and the Taft administration were betraying the conservation movement to large corporations. Pinchot took up Glavis's cause and gave secret Forest Service information to the muckrakers in order to expose Ballinger's rejection of conservation. The muckrakers, in turn, delivered some of their material to insurgent Republican senators like La Follette and Dolliver. *McClure's,* for example, gave La Follette everything it had unearthed by December 1909.

In early 1910 Pinchot sent a letter damning Ballinger and Taft, which Dolliver read on the Senate floor. Taft promptly fired Pinchot. Insurgents then forced a congressional investigation of the Interior Department. Although the committee's majority (carefully chosen by Republican leaders) exonerated Ballinger, the muckrakers and insurgents rallied behind the minority position brilliantly developed by Louis D. Brandeis, an insurgent lawyer hired by *Collier's Weekly* to vindicate Pinchot and Glavis. Brandeis showed, in effect, that Taft had lied in part of his attack on Pinchot and Glavis. La Follette proclaimed that Pinchot's fight was "the people's fight," and insurgents and muckrakers used the controversy to show that Taft was merely a tool of corporations.

By 1910, insurgent Republicans, like the muckrakers, were coming to believe that politics was narrowing into a struggle between the people and Privilege. Beveridge wrote Bristow and Bourne in July that "party lines all over the country have pretty well disappeared." The cause was clearly "the cheaper magazines which are circulating among the people and which have become the people's literature [producing] almost a mental and moral revolution among the people." Conservatives agreed that cooperation between insurgent journalists and politicians was destroying the traditional patterns of politics. Senator Boies Penrose of Pennsylvania blasted La Follette for deciding to cancel an appointment he had made to address the august Senate so that he could instead go "openly abroad upon the streets consulting with the editors of yellow journals and the agents of uplift magazines."

La Follette's reelection campaign in 1910 revealed the unity that had developed among the insurgents. Since everyone recognized that La Follette was the national insurgent leader and that his roll call campaigns were rapidly replacing incumbent conservative Republican senators with insurgents, Taft and the national party worked hard to defeat La Follette. The heart of the campaign in Republican Wisconsin was the September primary election, which would nominate candidates for the legislature that would elect a senator in early 1911.

Early in 1910 La Follette carefully rebuilt his organization by seeking La Follette clubs in each of the state's two thousand townships and precincts and by collecting the names of seven loyal insurgent Republicans and three loyal insurgent Democrats from each precinct. The basic problem was to persuade legislative candidates that they should pledge to vote for La Follette. He and his manager Charles Crownhart recruited friends to run in some districts, and they begged or intimidated candidates to withdraw in others where more than one insurgent candidate meant the probable election of an anti–La Follette legislator. Crownhart explained that "No one can really claim to be a good friend of Senator La Follette or the progressive cause, who by staying in the field in such a crisis, helps to defeat the cause of Senator La Follette." He and La Follette were pleased when candidates like Stephen Gruenheck ran La Follette's picture on the top of his campaign literature and Henry Krumrey called himself "the La Follette candidate for member of the Assembly."

La Follette's reelection campaign showed that the same insurgent spirit that had united prohibitionist Bristow with drinker Clapp in the 1909 Senate also prevailed among the voters. Although the Anti-Saloon League mounted a tremendous campaign to elect "dry" legislators in 1910 and tried to force La Follette to take a stand on the liquor question, La Follette replied that it was irrelevant to insurgency. He encouraged both "wet" and "dry" legislative candidates so long as they pledged to reelect him in 1911.

But the most remarkable features of the campaign were the 108 Wisconsin speeches given by insurgents from all over the country and the great prominence given La Follette's reelection in the popular magazines. "I believe that La Follette's success in this fight is the most important in American politics today," wrote Dolliver. La Follette had become seriously ill with a gallstone attack during the campaigning season, and the insurgents stepped in to replace him when he had to have the gallstones removed at the Mayo Clinic. Senators Borah, Bristow, Clapp, Cummins, and Dolliver, and Congressman George W. Norris gave speeches in Wisconsin. Prosecutor Francis J. Heney came from San Francisco, and direct-democracy champion George L. Record from New Jersey. Denver's Democratic juvenile judge Ben Lindsey spoke. Pinchot and fellow Roosevelt conservationist James R. Garfield gave speeches. Muckrakers Ray Stannard Baker, Steffens, S. S. Mc-

Clure, and Norman Hapgood guaranteed that the popular press would echo the case. They succeeded! La Follette's legislative supporters carried every county in the state and 1929 of the state's 2042 voting precincts. When Republicans easily won the general election of 1910, the legislature sent La Follette back to the Senate for a second term.

During his first term La Follette had emerged as the most prominent national spokesman and leader of the rapidly-growing insurgent group. Helping to define the role of consumer protest in transforming old issues, La Follette had shaken the conservative bastion of the Senate to its foundations and had forced his political party to divide along ideological lines. One of the most prominent 1910 beneficiaries of the insurgent movement, Governor-elect Hiram Johnson of California, expressed the insurgents' attitude toward La Follette: "A humble admirer and follower congratulates the PIONEER in the great progressive movement upon a deserved victory. You have been our inspiration."

V

Presidential Politics and the Tragedy of Insurgency

1911–1912

THE FUTURE of insurgency looked limitless after the elections of 1910. A political revolution had toppled the once omnipotent conservative Republican rulers of the nation and had united voters as consumers, taxpayers, and citizens across class and ethnic barriers. But the movement had been subtly transformed. Created by the extraordinary indignation of voters demanding that the political process be democratized in radically new ways, insurgency ran afoul of the ordinary ambition of the skilled politicians who spoke in its name at the national level. By 1912 the leaders' ambitions would degenerate into a bitter clash between La Follette and Roosevelt and, as a consequence, to division and demoralization throughout the ranks of insurgency.

The elections of 1910 suggested, as Kansas newspaper editor William Allen White wrote, that "never before have we been so nearly one people, with one dominant political ideal." Seven conservative Republican senators lost their seats, and the Republicans lost their majority in the House of Representatives for the first time since 1892. "Insurgency," wrote Ray Stannard Baker, "has ceased to be a mere uprising of guerrillas; it has become a great, a well-regulated, a self-conscious . . . movement." Democrats had gained seats not because their candidates had raised effective issues, but because insurgent Republicans had demolished conservative Republicans, as Republican President Taft and Democrat Louis Brandeis both acknowledged.

Insurgency gave voters a sense of emancipation from a hostile establishment dominated by corporations and political bosses. Ben Lindsey recalled his feeling after Denver had reelected him in 1908 despite corporation control over both established parties, "I went to bed that night, no longer a slave among slaves, but a freedman in a community that had at last risen against its masters and given them a warning of the wrath to come." But, as in the emancipation of the slaves, it was never clear exactly what liberation meant.

When insurgents emphasized common roles as consumers, taxpayers, and citizens, they lacked the older ethnic, class, and partisan constituencies that had traditionally defined programs. At the local level consumers knew exactly what they wanted — healthful water or lower taxes. But at the national level voters had difficulty knowing when the Money Trust or The System had been busted. They depended on strong leaders to define the issues. Reflecting the messianic role voters gave national insurgent leaders, a Jamestown, New York, lawyer wrote La Follette that he was "the MAN, the strong man, the leader of the way." So abstract had issues and programs become that a Lyle, South Dakota, resident asked La Follette to "let us know who are the people's friends and enemies." The decreasing immediacy of issues to voters and the increasing importance of leaders' election victories were insurgency's greatest weaknesses as it moved from the local to the national level.

La Follette knew when he returned to Washington on December 3, 1910, that insurgents across the country expected him to organize the movement into a united whole. During December he discussed the best format with journalists like

Steffens and Baker, publicists like U'Ren, politicians like Clapp and Bristow, and wealthy supporters like Spreckels and Crane. To La Follette, always haunted by financial fears, the basic need was money. When Rudolph Spreckels, the son of a sugar baron, and E. Clarence Jones, a Wall Street financier, each pledged $25,000 a year for five years, La Follette was ready to act. He decided that the organization should be Republican because congressional insurgent Republicans refused to identify with a third party. Leaning on U'Ren for advice, he prepared a program of state laws for direct election of senators, direct primary nominations, initiative, referendum and recall, corrupt practices acts, and, most important to him, direct election of delegates to presidential nominating conventions. The program thus aimed to create state organizations that would promote direct policymaking by voters and control their state's delegations to the presidential nominating convention in 1912.

He mailed the proposal to prominent insurgents over the Christmas vacation, and when he received their endorsements, he prepared to launch the National Progressive Republican League. He chose the NPRL officers carefully. Senator Jonathan Bourne of Oregon would be the president because he was prominently identified with direct democracy in that pioneering state and because he was rich. Congressman George W. Norris of Nebraska would be first vice-president because he led the House insurgents. Governor Chase S. Osborn of Michigan was second vice-president and a link to the insurgent governors. Bathtub magnate Charles R. Crane would be treasurer and, La Follette hoped, a major contributor. La Follette had formal endorsements from nine senators (his old insurgent friends Bourne, Beveridge, Bristow, Cummins, and Clapp, as well as Norris Brown of Nebraska, Joseph M. Dixon of Montana, Asle Gronna of North Dakota, and himself), sixteen congressmen, four governors, and such prominent publicists as Ray Stannard Baker, William Allen White, Gifford

Pinchot, George L. Record, James Garfield, William U'Ren, and Louis Brandeis.

He formally created the NPRL at his home on January 21, 1911. Proclaiming that "the will of the people shall be the law of the land," Senators La Follette, Bourne and Clapp and league Secretary Fred Howe encouraged the formation of NPRL chapters in all the states. State chapters would press their legislatures to enact the league's program of direct democracy in 1911 and then use the new democratic machinery to challenge President Taft's renomination in 1912. In California, for example, La Follette persuaded a reluctant Hiram Johnson to steer a direct presidential primary through that state's legislature and expected Johnson to lead California's challenge to Taft.

Such early successes, however, did not camouflage the internal dissension that gripped the league from its start. Pinchot and Garfield believed that Bourne was too lazy and Howe too vague. But the most demoralizing feature of the NPRL, the problem that nagged most constantly at La Follette, was the absence of Theodore Roosevelt from its ranks. Differences of temperament, ideology, and political style divided Roosevelt from La Follette and intensified their clashing ambitions to become president. Roosevelt refused to endorse the NPRL because he believed that the voters were incapable of ruling directly, and he preferred to work within the representative structure of government. Whereas La Follette favored vigorous busting of monopolies, Roosevelt believed that monopolies were inevitable and their behavior, not their size, should be regulated.

La Follette, who instinctively enjoyed raising public issues more than uniting legislative majorities behind bills, fully understood what Roosevelt meant when he rejected the NPRL because "I wish to follow in the path of Abraham Lincoln rather than in the path of John Brown and Wendell Phillips." La Follette was a radical idealist; Roosevelt was a wise practical politician. But since they both talked about disciplining corporate arrogance and since both had angered businessmen and conservative politicians in the past, both seemed part of the same movement to voters and insurgent politicians. La Follette believed that Roosevelt was waiting to see whether the NPRL could generate enough support to deny Taft the 1912 nomination.

The differences between Roosevelt and La Follette highlighted the problem of defining the terms "progressive" and "insurgent." Roosevelt defined *insurgents* as progressives who were "exceeding the speed limit," too radical. The term *progressive* covered a broad range of reformers, politicians, and interest groups seeking change. Insurgency connoted exposure of those in power by those outside, while progressivism more often applied to the activities of reformers in power. Insurgents had a more democratic faith in direct rule by voters, a greater skepticism toward the organization of voters into economic units, and a deeper moral outrage against large-scale industrial capitalism. Before 1910, when real national power resided in the united conservative leadership in Congress and the presidency, reformers like La Follette who had emphasized exposure and publicity were considered insurgents. After 1910, when reformers held the balance of power and secured several laws, they were often called progressives.

La Follette believed that the insurgent Republicans' position as the bloc holding the balance of power between regular Republicans and Democrats gave him a unique opportunity to establish a reputation as a statesman, which would offset Roosevelt's appeal and sharpen the differences between him and Taft. La Follette was clearly the leader of the thirteen insurgent Republican Senators. Clapp, Cummins, Bourne, Borah, Brown, Bristow, Crawford, and La Follette were joined in 1911 by Dixon, Gronna, William Kenyon of Iowa, Miles Poindexter of Washington, and John Works of California. They demonstrated their independence early in the session by giving their votes for president pro tem to Clapp and thereby prevented either Republicans or Democrats from electing their candidates, leaving the Senate without a president pro tem for a year and a half.

In 1911, La Follette found an issue that accented the changes in the Senate that he had achieved since 1906. William Lorimer, the "Blond Boss" of Illinois, had been elected by his legislature to a Senate seat in 1909 amid charges that he had bribed the legislators, and early in 1911 Taft had pressured enough Republicans for the Senate to seat Lorimer by a 46-to-40 vote. When a committee of the Illinois legislature reported new evidence of bribery, La Follette forced the Senate in June 1911 to launch a new investigation whose report thirteen months later led the Senate to unseat Lorimer by a 55-to-28 vote. Using the Lorimer investigation as one more example of how he had annihilated the Senate's Old Guard, La Follette persuaded the Senate to approve direct election of senators.

Believing that the insurgents were trying to destroy his administration, Taft tried in 1911 to undermine their support among popular magazines and consumers. He tried to drive the magazines out of business by raising their postal rates, and he sought support from the more conservative newspapers with a plan that would show that he was also a consumer champion. He prepared a treaty with Canada that would drop all tariff duties on such Canadian products as wheat, sheep, cattle, and the wood pulp and print paper from which newsprint was made. It would mean lower meat prices for American consumers and cheaper raw materials for the newspapers, which rallied behind the plan.

La Follette led the insurgent attack on Canadian reciprocity, charging that Taft had singled out the western farmers and ranchers for punishment by cheap Canadian competition. When the newspapers denounced La Follette and the insurgents for hypocritically defending high tariffs, La Follette conceived a brilliant way to restore the insurgents' credibility as consumer champions. He would amend the treaty by including lower duties on wool and cotton. La Follette and ten other insurgent Republicans repeatedly pressed for the wool and cotton amendments, but they failed because Taft threatened to veto the whole treaty if it were amended. Taft won his unamended treaty from the Senate, but the Canadians rejected it. And La Follette partially restored the insurgents' reputation as consumer champions by securing enough Democratic votes in July 1911 to enact laws that lowered duties on cotton, wool, and products purchased by farmers. When Taft vetoed these laws, he lost any advantage he had won as a consumer champion by promoting Canadian reciprocity.

Sensing that the issue of Canadian reciprocity had muddied the ideological waters, La Follette pushed another program that would restore his insurgent reputation. The Ballinger-Pinchot affair had drawn public attention to Alaska as a place where government could innovate policies in resource development and transportation. Guggenheim and Morgan interests were demanding private development of railroads and coal lands. After conferring with Brandeis, La Follette on August 19, 1911, introduced a resolution that explained his Alaskan policy. The government should lease mineral lands, collect rent on them, and require operators to provide adequate wages and safety for workers. The government should own one large coal mine to provide a yardstick for determining how cheaply coal could be produced, and it should require private mines to charge that price. Finally, the government should own the railroads, utilities, wharves, docks, and steamship lines. La Follette's motive in his first championship of government ownership was not opposition to private enterprise as such, but opposition to the special privileges by which railroads and coal companies became monopolies. Since competition was impossible because Alaskan exploitation would take large amounts of capital, La Follette favored government ownership to prevent special privileges.

On August 19, 1911, La Follette also introduced in a bill his comprehensive plan to regulate monopolies and corporations.

He had been present in the Supreme Court chambers four months earlier when in the Standard Oil case the Court had required the government to develop a new policy toward trusts. The Court had interpreted the Sherman Act as prohibiting only "unreasonable" conspiracies in restraint of trade. La Follette met Justice John Marshall Harlan (who had dissented) at his streetcar stop, and the two of them agreed that the decision was an outrageous judicial usurpation of Congress's intent. After failing to persuade Congress to legalize the principle of monopoly, the Money Trust had managed to get what it wanted from the Court, La Follette told newsmen.

The bill that La Follette introduced in August represented a collective effort by Brandeis, Congressman Irvine Lenroot, Francis Heney, John R. Commons, and Senators Bourne and Clapp. The bill added six provisions to the Sherman Act. It shifted the burden of proving what constituted an "unreasonable" restraint of trade from the government to the corporation whose activities had been questioned. The bill also guaranteed automatic damages to the victim of any "unreasonable" monopoly practice, whether the victims were consumers, producers, or both. Furthermore, the wrongdoing corporation was required to break up, and not merely regroup in friendly hands, as Standard Oil and other corporations had done in 1911. It specified several "unfair or oppressive" methods that would be "unreasonable" by definition, including rebates and pools. (Brandeis dissented from its provision that it was automatically "unreasonable" for any corporation to control 40 per cent of its market.) Through the bill ran the themes of restoring the discipline of the competitive market and fixing personal responsibility for wrongdoing. But no bill would restore competition, La Follette believed, when presidents like Roosevelt and Taft refused to prosecute zealously and now endorsed the Court's Standard Oil decision.

When the session adjourned on August 22, 1911, Ray Stannard Baker wrote that La Follette had been the dominant senator. He had rallied reformers to use their balance-of-power position to enact the wool bill, direct election of senators, and the farmers' free list. He had prevented Taft from discrediting the insurgents as consumer champions. His bills and resolutions formed a platform that established his position as a constructive statesman. It was a good record on which to seek the Republican presidential nomination.

As the presidential campaign began, the distance between the national and the local insurgents became clear. In the Canadian reciprocity debate La Follette and the insurgents would have helped consumers when they bought clothes, but hurt them when they bought bread and meat. La Follette's opposition to the bread and meat consumer, explained an insurgent club in Portland, Oregon, had "taken the wind out of our sails" as leaders for a La Follette-for-President campaign. Crusaders against local utilities in Los Angeles and Minneapolis protested loudly when La Follette endorsed statewide utility regulation laws in Minnesota and California because the utilities were trying to escape militant local movements by appealing to the more conservative state level. His endorsements amounted to condemnation of local insurgents. La Follette withdrew the endorsements, but his error showed how far rhetoric and national focus could diverge from the original sources of the movement.

La Follette's thoughts centered not on local insurgents but on the threat Roosevelt posed to his presidential campaign. Since progressives who admired both La Follette and Roosevelt agreed that a La Follette candidacy was the best way to hold the progressives together in the summer and fall of 1911, La Follette launched his campaign. Haunted by the fear that such prominent NPRL members as Gifford Pinchot and James Garfield were using him as a stalking horse for Roosevelt, La Follette again leaned heavily on his Wisconsin lieutenants. He brought Walter Houser from Wisconsin to head the campaign and sent his Wisconsin organizers into the other states.

By late summer most progressives believed that it would be

a straight fight between La Follette and Taft for the nomination. On September 7 the Minnesota Progressive Republican
convention endorsed La Follette. Ben Lindsey, after a lecture
tour of California, told Hiram Johnson that La Follette would
beat Taft there by five or ten to one, and Miles Poindexter
assured La Follette that he would carry Washington by five to
one. On October 16 the NPRL convened a Progressive Republican convention in Chicago, which unanimously endorsed La
Follette. The momentum was clearly moving in La Follette's
direction.

By any orthodox political manual La Follette should have
stumped the country in the fall, but instead he spent several of
the most crucial fall weeks of his campaign writing his autobiography between conferences! His personal desire to vindicate a pure record, a need for money that attracted him to the
American's offer of $12,000 for ten installments, and the belief
that the autobiography would win votes led him to do so.

He hoped that the autobiography would revolutionize popular attitudes toward the type of president voters wanted in
the same way that the roll call campaign had changed attitudes toward the Senate. He would show that he, like his
readers, had lived in sin and ignorance until he suddenly
discovered how special privileges dominated public life, and
he assumed that his readers would vicariously share his sense
of discovery and feel grateful for his battles. So converted, the
Republican rank-and-file would be inspired to overthrow their
masters. "Every line of this autobiography," he explained, "is
written for the express purpose of exhibiting the struggle for a
more representative government which is going forward in this
country, and to cheer on the fighters for that cause."

The autobiography had the desired effect. Albert J. Beveridge reported that it was "being read by millions of people"
and was "producing a profound impression." "In no other
way than that you have adopted," wrote a magazine reader
from Massachusetts, "could the dangers of our situation and
the necessity for concentrated action be so effectively brought

home to our people in every walk of life and of every degree of intelligence." The decision to write the autobiography was a "happy inspiration" that would stimulate a new political unity across class and ethnic lines. Ray Stannard Baker, who, along with John R. Commons, had helped La Follette on the autobiography, believed that it had guaranteed La Follette's presidential nomination. The autobiography was the high point of popular support for his presidential campaign, but it was also, as events would prove, his undoing among political leaders.

Many progressive politicians believed that La Follette had wasted his momentum. They believed that the nomination was his if he would only stump the country and organize his campaign better, and a meeting of Taft's supporters in the Republican National Committee confirmed that belief when it adjourned in utter demoralization at the president's chances for renomination. Progressive politicians grew increasingly impatient during the fall with La Follette's refusal to follow the traditional steps of presidential candidates. His manager in Oregon complained that La Follette was ignoring his perfect opportunity and was not providing that state with the leadership it needed. By late fall Garfield, Pinchot, and *Chicago Tribune* publisher Medill McCormick argued that La Follette had lost his chance and that Roosevelt was now the only candidate who could beat Taft. As criticism of his campaign by progressive politicians mounted steadily, La Follette and Walter Houser, his campaign manager, became increasingly depressed by the "Roosevelt situation" and feared NPRL betrayals of the senator's campaign.

By the time La Follette hit the campaign trail over the Christmas holidays it was probably too late to prevent Roosevelt from running. Although La Follette drew large and enthusiastic crowds in the crucial eastern Midwest as he denounced Taft, reporters often speculated that Roosevelt would have drawn still larger crowds. He disappointed many audiences because bad weather delayed his trains. In a speech at Lansing, Michigan, Governor Chase Osborn, a NPRL vice-president, began his introduction of La Follette by calling upon the senator to abandon his candidacy and endorse Roosevelt. But La Follette continued to hope that the voters were not as impressed by "practical" politics as Roosevelt's supporters.

The high point of his stumping campaign came at Carnegie Hall on January 22, 1912, when the reserves from two police stations had to be called out to control the thousands upon thousands who tried to get inside. La Follette quickly established rapport with the audience and never lost it, throwing aside his speech, and appearing as the fearless leader of the progressive movement. Observing that the audience was "made up of men and women from every walk of life," the *New York Times* reported that "Carnegie Hall never held a bigger nor a more enthusiastic audience."

La Follette hoped that his enthusiastic reception in New York might persuade Roosevelt to stay out of the race, but he learned at a dinner party after the speech that Roosevelt would soon declare his candidacy. At a meeting of the NPRL in Washington on January 29, publisher Medill McCormick, journalist Gilson Gardner, and Gifford Pinchot and his brother Amos urged La Follette to withdraw and support Roosevelt. La Follette refused, charging that these four had betrayed him. The four Roosevelt supporters promptly left the meeting, but the others encouraged La Follette to continue.

Driven frantic by months of hard work, his fears of betrayal now realized in fact, La Follette was not prepared for the news that his daughter Mary would need an operation on February 3 to remove a gland near the jugular vein. He knew, as his friends advised him, that he needed a rest, but the demon within him demanded that he press harder. Fearing that to cancel a speech would imply that he had conceded, La Follette decided to give his promised speech to the Periodical Publishers Association banquet in Philadelphia on the evening before Mary's operation. He decided to give his usual speech attacking private monopoly and special interests, and to please the audience of magazine publishers by contrasting their great service to insurgency through the muckraking movement with the subservience of daily newspapers to special interests.

La Follette walked into the banquet hall about 11:00 P.M. as Governor Woodrow Wilson of New Jersey was concluding a brief and graceful speech to the overfed, bored audience. La Follette had been too nervous to eat all day and had taken a shot of whiskey before the speech. He began by condescendingly apologizing for using a manuscript and lost the audience at that point. La Follette reacted to rude listeners by aggressively compelling them to pay attention. He lost his temper, angrily shook a finger at disrespectful guests, and listeners walked out on him. He stopped reading the manuscript, digressed for several minutes, then resumed without realizing that he had just made the same point in his digression. The audience hooted derisively at his rhetorical questions. La Follette lost complete sense of time, rambling on for two hours. Worse, La Follette had not known that the banquet's purpose was to reconcile newspapers with magazines.

The next morning Americans awoke to read in their newspapers that La Follette had suffered a nervous breakdown. The *Washington Post* quoted La Follette's "friends" that the senator was withdrawing his candidacy. Realizing that he had been under a "long nervous strain," La Follette said privately that he only needed a little rest.

Why did the newspapers use a poor speech and nervous manner to disqualify La Follette for the presidency? Of course, he had bored and insulted listeners who could fight him in their newspapers. But more importantly, wealthy newspaper publishers saw La Follette as a genuine menace to large-scale industrial capitalism. The *Baltimore Sun* complained that La Follette's hated "community of interest" included not only newspapers but all job-oriented groups — businessmen, farmers, workers — that depended on a market economy: "The community of interests which the Wisconsin Senator attacks is the very marrow of our civilization. To attain his glorious isolation, Mr. La Follette must seek out the solitudes of the forest and the haunts of primeval man." La Follette was too critical of capitalism and materialism, charged the *Washington Evening Star;* he was obsessed by a vision of finding "the dollar mark plainly stamped upon the backs of officials and the pages of statute books." Perhaps the newspapers reacted so violently because they knew, as an editorial writer for the *Philadelphia Evening Telegraph* assured him, that his charge against the newspapers was correct.

La Follette's supporters — Bourne, Bristow, Lenroot, Clapp, Houser, and Ohio manager John D. Fackler — urged him to withdraw on February 5, but La Follette refused and announced that he would still "make an aggressive contest" for the nomination. At the same time, however, George L. Record, chairman of the October conference that had "nominated" La Follette, declared that Houser had told him that La Follette had withdrawn, and five days later Gifford Pinchot sent a widely publicized telegram to the Minnesota Progressive Republican League: "In my judgment La Follette's condition such that further serious candidacy impossible."

The "breakdown" and "collapse" clearly bothered the political leaders far more than the voters, who simply did not understand the conflicting statements about La Follette's candidacy. A poll of the *Kansas City Star*'s readers showed no change in La Follette's support after the Philadelphia speech. As most polls revealed that Roosevelt was the most popular candidate before as well as after La Follette's speech, local progressive leaders seized the "breakdown" as the excuse to shift support from La Follette to Roosevelt. Arguing that La Follette was now "unavailable," John D. Fackler steered Cleveland's Progressive Republicans to Roosevelt, who could win. J. C. Heald, a La Follette supporter, protested that Roosevelt was not even a progressive: "Nominate Roosevelt and all you have to do is to take a pair of eyeglasses and four teeth and you'll have a platform sufficient to elect him. . . . Away with principles."

La Follette could now return to the free-swinging style that he had stifled earlier to please conflicting progressive leaders. He did not enjoy working with independent people like Pinchot who were his equals. His closest friend, Gilbert Roe, could see that La Follette was now a free man again; Roosevelt's formal announcement and the desertions by his supporters were "letting you out of a good deal of responsibility."

La Follette now attacked Roosevelt instead of Taft. The "Interests" were so alarmed by the popular support for La Follette's candidacy, he argued, that they had promoted Roosevelt in order to destroy the genuinely insurgent movement. Roosevelt had presided over the spectacular growth of holding companies as president, and now such prominent associates of J. P. Morgan as George W. Perkins, Frank Munsey, and E. H. Gary were rewarding him by financing his campaign. Had La Follette been president from 1901 to 1909, he would have fired any U.S. District Attorney who had failed to enforce the antitrust law. La Follette insisted that he was clearly the more consistent progressive. He repeatedly challenged Roosevelt to divulge the amounts contributed by big businessmen to his campaign, for, La Follette charged, Roosevelt was their greatest ally.

So bitterly did La Follette attack the Roosevelt leaders in the NPRL — Pinchot, Garfield, McCormick, and Hiram Johnson — for deserting his candidacy that they defied Roosevelt's orders and attacked the Wisconsin senator. La Follette had feared Roosevelt's candidacy since he had announced his own; he was glad that he was now free to wage his own kind of campaign.

La Follette believed that his only hopes of defying Roosevelt and reviving his flagging campaign were the nation's historic first two presidential primary elections in North

Dakota in late March and Wisconsin in early April. He had lectured often in North Dakota, had championed that state's wheat farmers in the Canadian reciprocity debate, and had the support of that state's Congressman Helgesen and Senator Gronna. On March 12 he began a four-day speaking tour there. The *Minneapolis Tribune's* correspondent reported that "the Wisconsin senator looks anything but a sick man. He is tense, vigorous and full of fighting ire." La Follette won the North Dakota primary with 58 per cent of the vote, compared with 39 per cent for Roosevelt and 3 per cent for Taft. On April 2 La Follette buried Taft in Wisconsin by a three-to-one margin, and Roosevelt received only 628 votes. The *Denver Express* read "a vindication of popular government" into the North Dakota results: "The people go on when leaders falter — . . . the religion of civic righteousness has so seized upon the voters of this country that no cowardice of leaders, not half-heartedness that is more deadly than opposition, can stop the progress of great reforms which shall bring about a new era of equality and freedom."

La Follette campaigned in Nebraska, Oregon, and California to enthusiastic crowds, but the progressive Republican leaders of these states were firmly supporting Roosevelt, including NPRL leaders like George W. Norris in Nebraska, Hiram Johnson and most of his California supporters, and NPRL President Jonathan Bourne in Oregon. Roosevelt easily won these primaries, as well as one in Illinois. La Follette consoled himself with his second place finishes in Nebraska, Oregon, and South Dakota primaries.

The Roosevelt–La Follette conflict very nearly wrecked progressive movements on the local and state level. Congressman George W. Norris, leader of the House insurgents who had slashed the Speaker's powers, was running for the Senate from Nebraska and hoped his state's delegation to the national convention would vote to unseat Taft. He had urged La Follette to run, but when a Roosevelt boom developed in Nebraska he tried to reconcile the Roosevelt and La Follette organizations. Roosevelt's organization threatened to run a candidate for the Senate against Norris unless Norris would support Roosevelt, so Norris decided to compromise by running pictures of both La Follette and Roosevelt on his literature. La Follette then telegraphed Norris to remove his name and picture from any union with Roosevelt's. The secretary of the La Follette League of Nebraska pleaded with La Follette to change his mind because his decision meant "an almost certain victory for the reactionary element of the party." After La Follette refused to support a united anti-Taft slate of delegates to the convention, a reluctant Norris supported Roosevelt. Wisconsin Congressman Lenroot privately sympathized with Norris's dilemma. Similarly, when La Follette spent three weeks in California roasting Hiram Johnson and his followers for their betrayal, Johnson feared that the conservative Southern Pacific machine would return to power and "the great movement in the State would be wrecked upon a rotten collateral issue." In the end, Roosevelt, Norris, and Johnson were strong enough in Nebraska and California to prevent conservative victories.

Although La Follette had only 41 delegates to the Republican convention that met at Chicago in June (Wisconsin, North Dakota, and five from South Dakota), he used them so that "the Bluffer shall be kept as far from the wire as possible." He saw treachery within his own delegation when Wisconsin Governor Francis E. McGovern accepted Roosevelt's overtures to serve as temporary chairman. But he was not disturbed when the convention ultimately renominated Taft, nor was he attracted to the Roosevelt followers who bolted Taft's nomination and formed a Progressive Party to nominate their hero. He realized, along with dispassionate observers like Democrat Woodrow Wilson, that his fight with Roosevelt had been the most important factor in depriving Roosevelt of the Republican nomination. He had indeed kept the Bluffer from the wire.

La Follette spent the summer and fall of 1912 vindicating

his course. In Senate speeches, magazine editorials, and three new chapters of his autobiography, La Follette documented Roosevelt's betrayal of the progressive movement beginning with his smothering of La Follette's conservation and railroad bills in 1907 and culminating in his 1912 indebtedness to the House of Morgan. Although La Follette did not endorse any candidate in 1912, his magazine clearly preferred Wilson. But he questioned Wilson because, as he wrote his son Robert, "I have had some experience with raw progressives who haven't shed their milk teeth – quite recent experiences too. Hence I shall watch their eighteen month old [D]emocratic progressive perform a little." La Follette's supporters probably split their votes between Wilson, Socialist Eugene Debs, and, to a lesser degree, Roosevelt.

The struggle between La Follette and Roosevelt that ended in Wilson's victory destroyed the promise of insurgency that had seemed so bright in November 1910. H. N. Rickey, editor-in-chief of the five insurgent Scripps-McRae newspapers in Ohio, maintained that "from a journalistic standpoint the situation is about as difficult as I have ever known in politics." Never again in the twentieth century would progressives come so close to capturing the GOP as they had in 1911 before the split.

In the end, two ambitious politicians wrecked the movement they had both played such important parts in directing at the national level. La Follette's refusal to accept joint anti-Taft delegate slates deserved the censure he received from Norris and Johnson. Roosevelt's threat to run candidates against Norris and Gronna was equally reprehensible. Their joint rejection of the proposal by respected mutual friends Senator Clapp and Congressman William Kent of California that La Follette tackle Taft in the "La Follette belt" from Lake Michigan across the northern plains while Roosevelt tackled Taft in other areas revealed the depth of their bitterness.

Lincoln Steffens saw clearly what was happening. "The

progressive movement in this presidential campaign has been suffering from old-time political methods." In this movement whose greatest asset was the feeling of participation it gave voters, "the leaders met, discussed plans and reached decisions; they met again and unmade the previous decisions, got together and split, all in good faith, but in private. The public has not been let into the confidence of this new democratic movement" with the result that "the leaders have been working the situation out with no direct pressure of an enlightened public opinion, and therefore no public support or correction." The problem was compounded because La Follette and Roosevelt saw themselves not as politicians, but as emancipators. "There is more danger of a division among men of principle than among a lot of party machinists," Steffens explained, because "it is easier to divide a dollar equitably, or even a lot of offices, than it is to divide a principle."

The personal clash exposed a tension within national insurgency between its leaders' quite ordinary aspirations, generated by the representative system of government, and the quite revolutionary thrust of the movement's rhetoric toward a system of direct democracy in which one day the people would rule directly without leaders, bosses, and machines. The clash revealed the inherent danger within insurgency as it moved from grassroots issues to an increasingly abstract and messianic national orientation.

But the result was clear. When insurgency degenerated into squabbles between politicians, voters lost their faith in the movement's ultimate triumph over large-scale industrial capitalism. Voters wondered whether there would be any salvation if the saviors turned out to be ordinary politicians. Belle La Follette sensed "something different" about the crowds in 1912. Debates after 1911 lacked the popular enthusiasm of the previous half-dozen years. Exposure of wrongdoing by corporations and conservative politicians was now irrelevant since the reform leaders also ignored the popular will. There would be no Armageddon, just amelioration and adjustment.

The meaning of 1912 for La Follette was clear. He was no

longer the leader of a powerful force in Congress. The congressional insurgents viewed him as a sick and vindictive man. But they were unable to create a new leader to fill the role La Follette had played from 1906 to 1911. Since the insurgent Republicans had generally better brains, greater vision, and more experience than the Democrats who were elected from 1908 to 1912 (as the Democrats had acknowledged by following the insurgents' legislative leads), the loss of an insurgent Republican leader meant that hereafter the president's influence on the shape of progressivism would be much greater than Congress's, with the further result that the people would be even less able to shape policy. Perhaps, in the end, the insurgents were simply guerrillas who were most effective when conservatives in their party ran the government. Once they had overthrown their enemies, the Aldriches and Tafts, they were left rudderless, adrift in a political world they had created but were unable to direct.

VI

Insurgency in
a Modernizing World
1913–1916

DURING THE WILSON YEARS the progressive movement developed fundamentally new shapes and directions. Old
appeals to the united community of consumers and taxpayers
gave way to narrower appeals to interest groups based on people's jobs. The old insurgent emphasis on direct majority rule
ebbed with the rise of experts and commissions. The shift away
from popular democracy weakened insurgency and rendered it
vulnerable to the growing power of interest groups and experts, to the rise of a new conservatism based on insurgents' old appeals, and to increasingly divisive issues based on
voters' ethnic and religious loyalties.

The election of 1912 had shattered the unity of insurgents
in Congress. La Follette and other insurgents still rejected the
large-scale corporation as an illegitimate product of greed and
special privilege and, inspired by consumer-taxpayer outlooks,
still promoted plans to redistribute wealth and power. They
still trusted exposure and publicity to accomplish their goals.
But during Wilson's first term they no longer cooperated as a
unified movement; they made a virtue of the "strong individuality and . . . elemental personal independence of character," as La Follette called it, that justified their working as

individuals. In a majoritarian world there was only the individual and the majority, and insurgents wanted people to resist all other loyalties. Senator John Works of California condemned any group discipline, whether caucus discipline over legislators, organized medicine's over doctors, or labor unions' over workers.

The frantic conferences among insurgents ceased, and the La Follettes withdrew into their supportive family life. Belle and Robert looked forward to drives in the country and the new motion pictures for release from the pressures of work. Belle was developing her own career as a popular suffragist speaker. The two teenaged boys had frequent parties that gave the house the merry atmosphere both parents loved. A few close friends, like Louis Brandeis, John R. Commons, or Seamen's Union President Andrew Furuseth, would join the family for occasional meals that often became working sessions.

At first La Follette had great hopes that Wilson would be an ally. During the 1912 campaign and the early months of 1913, the new president had echoed some insurgent ideas. He had even invited La Follette to the White House to suggest a program. It was not long, however, before Wilson abandoned cooperation with insurgents in favor of working through a tightly-organized Democratic caucus. Democrats debated each important measure in the caucus, trying to conciliate their party's conflicting factions. Once the caucus had voted on an issue, its members submerged their differences, supported the majority position, and presented a united front against both conservative and insurgent Republicans. To insurgents like La Follette the caucus was a new form of machine rule by a legislative minority. Roasting King Caucus in his magazine in July, La Follette argued that 26 Democratic senators, a majority of the party's 51 members, now controlled the Senate. The country now witnessed the legislative results of rigid party discipline among Democrats, which was in contrast to the uncompromising debates between insurgent and conservative Republicans.

Wilson, knowing that downward tariff revision had united most Democrats since the days of Thomas Jefferson, made passage of the Underwood-Simmons Tariff his first goal. Democratic members of the Finance Committee drafted it, received the approval of the Democratic caucus, and presented it to the Senate for the formality of a vote. Although the bill lowered many Payne-Aldrich duties to the level insurgent Republicans had wanted in 1909, the issue was so partisan that most insurgents voted against it. When Progressive Miles Poindexter and Republican La Follette cast the only non-Democratic votes for it, the *Philadelphia North American* observed that "La Follette's vote was undoubtedly based upon the exercise of greater intelligence, upon stronger convictions, and greater independence than that of any other vote cast."

The lower tariff necessitated new bases for government revenue, and the resulting debate over the income tax opened major ideological divisions. Conservative Republicans wanted to tax all incomes over $1000 so that most Americans would pay, but insurgents in both parties wanted to tax incomes over $3000 or $4000 so that the tax might redistribute wealth. Democratic leaders were less interested in this debate than in using the tax to raise revenue, and they reported a bill from the caucus that proposed a 1 per cent tax on incomes over $3000 and an additional surtax (the graduated feature) rising from 1 percent to 3 per cent on incomes over $100,000. Insurgent Republicans argued that these rates were inadequate to redistribute wealth. On August 27, 1913, La Follette climaxed their battle by proposing an amendment imposing a 10 per cent rate on incomes over $100,000, and Poindexter proposed 20 per cent on incomes over $1 million. Mississippi's John Sharp Williams, speaking for the Wilsonian Democrats, charged that the insurgents were less interested in raising revenue than in punishing the rich. But insurgent Democrats James Vardaman of Mississippi and James Reed of Missouri demanded that the caucus reconvene to consider the La Follette amendment. Wilson supported his party's leaders in a letter stating that "it is much safer to begin upon somewhat moderate lines." The caucus raised the rate on incomes over $100,000 to 7 per cent, a compromise between the bill's original 4 per cent and La Follette's 10 per cent. The Democratic income tax of 1913 thus occupied a middle ground, and insurgent Republicans deserved the credit for any component of social reform in the law.

Insurgent Republicans then challenged Wilson's program to regulate banking and currency by means of a Federal Reserve Board. They had too long believed that the Money Trust was the worst of all trusts to accept Wilson's proposal, which they believed would strengthen Wall Street's power. Insisting that "the greatest banks of the financial center . . . have become primarily agencies of promotion and speculation," La Follette argued that they formed a "community of interest" with the transportation and industrial corporations that they controlled. In September 1913 he blamed "stock ticker railroading" for a wreck on the New Haven and argued that the government should "put in jail the men who robbed and ruined the New Haven railroad by means of inside holding companies." J. P. Morgan's greatest sin, explained insurgent Ida Tarbell in the *American,* was his "ignorance of the relation between the great enterprises he conducted with such simple and magnificent self-confidence and the man who buys his coal by the basketful. . . . Morgan had little or no sense of a personage with whom the rich and powerful must at last deal fairly or fall, and that is the 'ultimate consumer.' " Consumers would again control business, insurgents argued, when the investment bankers no longer controlled large corporations and credit.

La Follette and other insurgents blamed Wilson's fear of offending big businessmen for the program's failure to attack the power of concentrated wealth. Big businessmen had tried to restrain politicians from enacting an insurgent program by raising the old fear that reform measures would produce an economic slump. U.S. Steel's E. H. Gary declared that "the gravest menace to this country" was that politicians "have so little at stake in the outcome of their acts that they are little affected if they turn prosperity into depression." La Follette believed that such charges frightened Wilson. "The Administration has been scared stiff for the last few weeks," he wrote Spreckels in late 1913. "Democratic leaders . . . are looking for a chance . . . to get cooperation between the big boys who have been doing bad things and the government."

In fact, Wilsonian Democrats had defined the basic problem as the need to create a flexible financial system to help businessmen and farmers in an expanding economy. The Federal Reserve Act provided mechanisms to mobilize bank reserves more freely and to regulate changes in the business cycle by controlling the amount of credit available to bankers to lend and by establishing a more flexible currency. Although some conservatives opposed the Federal Reserve Act because it gave the president, not bankers, power to control its members, insurgents opposed it because it did not attack the fundamental power of investment bankers. La Follette proposed that the bill abolish interlocking directorates, and Bristow proposed a publicly owned central bank. Wilson invoked caucus discipline to kill any alternative.

Wilson killed insurgent proposals, La Follette believed, because he feared that big businessmen would retaliate against reform laws, as they had in 1907, by stimulating a panic that would lead workers and farmers to vote the Democrats out. It had taken the Democrats twenty years to recover national power since the voters had blamed them for the depression of the 1890s. La Follette mocked Wilson for "having turned the Money Power over to the unrestrained fury of the Big Banking Interests."

By early 1914, La Follette thought, Wilson was committed to maintaining domestic prosperity by not offending big businessmen. And when Wilson appointed conservatives to administer the new Federal Reserve Board La Follette felt that his beliefs were confirmed. Wilson roasted insurgents for opposing his nominees. "We have breathed too long the air of suspicion and distrust," complained Wilson, when we should have "common understanding . . . for prosperity, the prosperity of co-operation and mutual trust and confidence." He never understood why insurgents opposed his nomination of a director of the International Harvester Corporation then under indictment for violating the antitrust law. But enough Democrats agreed with the insurgents to give him his first major defeat in July 1914, forcing him to withdraw his nominees.

The fight between insurgents and Wilsonians over the banking program and the income tax reflected a gradual but profound shift in the shape of the progressive movement during Wilson's first administration. Wilson and the majority Democrats brought to progressivism such different constituents and assumptions that the movement acquired a new direction — a direction that might be called modernization. As a label the term *modernization* lacks the coherence of *insurgency* because its adherents lacked the self-conscious unity of the insurgents and because Wilson had rhetorically rejected some of its assumptions during the campaign of 1912 and the early months of his presidency, but it still describes the basic process of change during his administration.

Modernizers accepted the inevitability of large-scale industrialism and — instead of joining the insurgents in challenging its assumptions of concentration, planning, and profit — they worked to help its victims. Some of their constituents derived their ideology from their daily lives as workers and recent immigrants. The insecurity of employment haunted them. Their consciousness of themselves as workers had been increased by nineteenth-century battles to impose on them such habits as punctuality and temperance and by the control they had lost when the new technology had deprived them of ownership of their tools. Many had turned to urban political machines and labor unions to help preserve their jobs and cultural habits. The modernizers' other constituents were the growing number of farmers who were becoming increasingly job-oriented in the 1910s as they formed new organizations to market their goods instead of working with other consumers to attack concentrated businesses.

The increasing tendency of farmers and workers to define their problems in ways that job-oriented pressure groups could solve, a tendency that gave progressivism its modernizing features, was an American form of two changes that were occurring throughout the industrializing West. Both changes originated not with workers but with industrialists.

From the beginning of industrialization in the eighteenth-century Brititsh textile industry, industrialists took generations to wear down the resistance of workers to the whole new patterns of life dictated by the machine and the factory. Rejecting these new disciplines at first, workers could hardly conceive of a job-oriented pressure group. As, over agonizing generations, farmers and workers came to learn that the safest and surest way to gain relief from their problems was, as it was for industrialists, through job-oriented action, they copied the industrialists. Industrialists had come to believe that competition with rivals was the greatest stumbling block to stable growth and profits as they faced the mounting costs of machinery. By the late nineteenth century they had developed methods like pools, trusts, and holding companies to limit competition. When workers and farmers formed job-oriented groups, they were basically copying the industrialists in their fundamental goal of limiting competition with other farmers and workers. The holding company that permitted industrialists to fix higher prices than a competitive market would have established was no different from the labor union that permitted workers to fix wages at higher levels than a competitive labor market would have established. Once organized bodies of industrialists, workers, and farmers had agreed on the need to limit competition and on the method of job-oriented pressure groups, they turned to governments to help them destroy competition and outflank more radical groups that refused to

accept the world that the industrialists had created. Modernizing progressivism in the United States had its counterparts in
Bismarck's Germany or late Victorian and Edwardian Britain,
where leaders promoted a new role for the state in ameliorating the insecurities of factory life in order to undercut the
appeal of socialist and insurgent movements.

Although modernization had evolved with industrialism
and immigration in the nineteenth century, its job-oriented
pressure groups acquired much greater national influence during the Democratic Wilson administration. The basic objective of these groups was to provide jobs for workers and
markets for farmers and businessmen through steady economic
growth, and their basic methods were adjustment and amelioration. Finding the Democrats receptive to their job-oriented
appeals, modernizers shunned the insurgents' enthusiasm for
exposure, prosecution, and direct majority rule.

Democratic modernizers cooperated with many businessmen
who by 1913 were concluding that they could best silence their
muckraking and insurgent critics and eliminate the ruinous
consequences of competition to their profits by regulating
themselves. Following the Supreme Court's 1911 distinction
between reasonable and unreasonable business practices, they
formed groups, like the United States Chamber of Commerce
in 1912, to decide fair and unfair methods and then secure
federal policing of their internal agreements. Elliott H. Goodwin, Chamber of Commerce general secretary, explained to La
Follette that businessmen now repudiated "the notorious
methods adopted by a small but powerful and prominent part
of business in the past." Goodwin emphasized the need for
accommodation: "We recognize three great fundamental economic forces — agriculture, labor, and commerce — and we
wish to cooperate with the other two as far as possible."
Delighted that businessmen shared the modernizers' faith in
economic growth and definition of citizens in terms of their
jobs, Wilson announced in 1914 that "the antagonism between business and government is over."

Modernization required the rapid national emergence of professionals trained in methods of accommodation. In the 1890s and early 1900s thousands of concerned amateurs wanted to narrow the chasm between rich and poor by improving the working and living environments of the poor. They moved into poor neighborhoods and worked with their new neighbors. Coming to believe that local problems could best be solved by state and national laws, they worked more and more with reformers from other cities and less and less with their poor neighbors, developing an awareness of themselves as professionals. Eventually, these experienced reformers tried to drive out the inexperienced by establishing state-sanctioned systems of certification and examination. They emphasized the values of professionalization: self-regulation, accommodation, stability, and a fear of majority rule. They worked with other groups to develop scientific and efficient plans to ameliorate industrial problems. The new professional journalists shunned the muckrakers' sensational exposures in favor of speculative theory and specific programs. Uninterested in reaching mass audiences or changing readers' world views, they assumed that the professional reform elite, not the majority, held real political power.

Under these pressures the progressive movement shifted direction rapidly and old ideas received new emphases. Identifying with their roles as producers, new groups of farmers and workers found a receptive hearing in the first Wilson Administration. In 1914 Congress exempted unions and farm organizations from antitrust prosecution, thus encouraging the organization of job-oriented groups of farmers and workers.

The farmers' movement aimed to destroy the middlemen — grain elevators, banks, and railroads — who deprived farmers of higher returns. Through groups like the Equity Society and later the Nonpartisan League, they wanted to "free the market" by creating cooperative exchanges or state-owned grain elevators, and they wanted the government to replace banks as their source of credit. As farmers sought greater rewards for their labor, they were no longer interested, as they had been in the 1900s, in direct democracy, tax reform, and the other concerns they had shared with other consumers and taxpayers.

La Follette came to see the change in farmers' outlooks between 1911 and 1914 from consumer to producer because his oldest insurgent friends in Minnesota and North Dakota — leaders like James Manahan and George S. Loftus of Minneapolis — had shifted during that time from spearheading broad programs of political reform to leading the campaign to organize wheat farmers. He saw through their eyes that farmers no longer looked at other consumers as allies in a struggle to discipline producers but instead merely as the people to consume farm products. Recognizing this rapid spread of farmer consciousness, La Follette created a special farm department in *La Follette's* magazine in November 1914, spoke to the movement's largest convention at St. Paul in December 1915, and warmly supported federal low-cost loans to farmers (passed in 1916) and exemption from antitrust laws for farm organizations (passed in 1914) .

By promoting the ideals of efficiency and service, the new professional reformers transformed not only the insurgents' ideas about farmers and consumers, but also their conceptions of community and democracy. La Follette's national fame rested heavily on the use of experts to administer Wisconsin's reform laws, a process hailed as the Wisconsin Idea. Although he was uneasy with some facets, he publicized the Wisconsin Idea in his magazine. The "social center" movement blossomed in Wisconsin under Edward J. Ward of the University of Wisconsin Extension Division. "Social center development is the construction of the necessary machinery whereby hitherto wasted civil and social forces may be coordinated [by a] social engineer," explained Ward in *The Social Center* (1913) . Prodded by the State Teachers Association and the University's extension division, the 1911 legislature enacted a law that allowed local schools to become social centers for educational and political discussions. By 1915 the state boasted over 500 such centers. These centers contrasted sharply with the clubs of the 1890s that had spawned insurgency. The original clubs had *assumed* a sense of community among the people from all classes who were trying to solve local and immediate problems, whereas the centers were promoted by professionals to *impose* citizenship and a sense of community. The centers depended on state direction and funds; the earlier clubs had done whatever their members wanted. The clubs of the 1890s had been formless democracy in action; the social centers were actionless democracy in form, the professional educators' attempt to impose ideals of community and democracy.

The most famous feature of the Wisconsin Idea was the Industrial Commission, created by the 1911 legislature. Inspired by economist John R. Commons, its most influential member, the commission regulated the working environment. Commons and the commission replaced Wisconsin's labor laws with codes prepared by experts. Commons believed that "leading representatives of conflicting interests" should determine conditions of labor without pressure from politicians or consumers. He tried to ensure job stability through collective bargaining contracts and to persuade employers that their largest self-interest lay in providing a safe, healthful environment for their workers. *La Follette's* carried Commons's boast that the commission system created a fourth branch of government that could base its decisions on investigation by experts of the work process in each industry, and the magazine hailed Ohio, Indiana, New York, and Colorado for adopting the Wisconsin solution. The expert, responsive to private job-oriented interest groups, was replacing the politician, responsive not only to interest groups but to mass, consumer-conscious movements.

While Commons was persuading La Follette to accept the importance of the state and the expert in ameliorating working conditions, another close friend, Louis Brandeis, was lead-

ing him to define the problem of monopoly in terms of
inefficient management, not consumer discipline. Believing
that "efficiency is the hope of democracy," as he wrote in *La
Follette's* in 1915, Brandeis argued that monopolistic corporate managements wasted money and men. Competition
would force corporations to make better products more
cheaply and efficiently and, as a result, to charge lower prices
and pay higher wages. Brandeis preferred the expert to the
corporate manager because the expert was motivated only by
dedication to service. The problem of monopoly was the problem of its efficiency, not its legitimacy, and the expert, not the
consumer, could best judge that efficiency. Profoundly influenced by Brandeis's argument, La Follette after 1913 gave
more and more emphasis to the inefficiency of corporate management.

Progressivism increasingly reflected these new assumptions:
first, job-oriented interest groups offered the best way to
achieve justice and democracy because one's place in the productive process, his job, was more important than community
loyalty. Secondly, waste caused injustice, and scientific and
professional techniques helped industrialism's victims while
increasing profits. Third, the expert, responsive to interest
groups, replaced the journalist, concerned with the reading
public as consumers and taxpayers, as definer of "the public
interest." Fourth, independent commissions were superior to
legislatures because they prized efficiency and science over the
politicians' blind subservience to the popular will. In short,
science replaced morality and democracy as the measure of an
individual's or group's threat to the community.

La Follette increasingly assisted the victims of capitalism
rather than attacking capitalists themselves. Instead of using
the exposure of the National Association of Manufacturers'
campaign to kill organized labor's bills in 1913 as a means to
attack the NAM, La Follette and other progressives used it to
demonstrate the need to support labor. *La Follette's* announced that congressmen now listened to Samuel Gompers
and the AFL. Realizing that consumer consciousness was

rapidly ebbing as a political force, La Follette understood that most support for labor laws now came from unions and modernizers. He championed an eight-hour-day for railroad workers in 1916 because shorter hours meant "stronger bodies, greater physical efficiency, a higher degree of mental alertness" and because workers in "less hazardous callings" had already achieved it. In contrast with his stand in 1907, he insisted in 1916 that railroad workers be permitted to work overtime and receive time and a half when they did it. Between 1907 and 1916 the issue of railroad hours had evolved from the consumers' right to discipline anyone who menaced their safety into a fight between labor and business.

Though he saw that the political climate was now more conducive to job-oriented groups, La Follette retained many insurgent qualities. He devoted more energy to exposing the railroads' efforts to buy public opposition to the eight-hour-law than he did to defending the unions' claims. He believed that organized labor was often so preoccupied by its own membership that it ignored the plight of working women and children. When some modernizers applauded time-and-motion studies and the assembly line as means of achieving more efficient production, La Follette charged that they were trying to "grind the last ounce of work out of the toilers" and persuaded the Senate in 1916 to defeat a provision in the army appropriations bill that sped up the assembly line.

La Follette's continuing concern for consumers is shown by his work on the Seamen's Act of 1915. Andrew Furuseth, the tall, stooped president of the Seamen's Union, had convinced La Follette in 1909 that the iron contracts which bound seamen to shipping companies constituted slavery. The law reflected Furuseth's concern for the seamen. It abrogated binding one-year contracts and allowed sailors to quit ships whenever their cargo was unloaded, and, in an attempt to give American sailors the jobs held by foreign sailors, it required that three-fourths of the crew speak English.

La Follette persuaded Furuseth to accept provisions to

benefit passengers as well as seamen, including the require-
ments that ships carry enough lifeboats for every passenger,
have enough experienced seamen for two to man every lifeboat, and stage lifeboat and fire drills. He promoted the bill as
a consumer protection measure for potential passengers who
could imagine the horror of drowning in a raging sea. Nearly
13,000 people had drowned in sea disasters between 1900 and
1914, and La Follette used each shipwreck to dramatize the
need for his law. The 1600 passengers who had lost their lives
on the *Titanic* in 1912 because the ship did not carry enough
lifeboats were "sacrificed to greed and avarice," he said, add-
ing, "Many call it murder."

La Follette introduced the seamen's bill in 1910 and every
subsequent session until it passed, but he found few enthusiastic supporters. Linking his bill to products consumers
bought more frequently, he found a "sordid indifference to
public health" among manufacturers and ship companies
alike. La Follette and Consumers' League head Florence
Kelley were likewise appalled when consumers failed to testify
for the bill. By threatening a filibuster against appropriations
bills, La Follette finally steered the Seamen's Act to passage
early in 1915. He and Furuseth had to beg a reluctant Wilson
to sign it.

The ship companies then played to the Wilsonians' fear of
business failures that would cause depressions by pressuring
Commerce Secretary William Redfield not to enforce the act's
discretionary provisions. The National Association of Manufacturers and the shipping companies contended that American shippers would fail if the act was enforced, and the Great
Northern, Pacific Mail, and Robert Dollar companies either
sold their ships or transferred them from American to British
registry. La Follette exposed "The Ship Owners' Conspiracy"
in his July 1915 magazine, charging that the *New York Times*
and *Journal of Commerce* were opposing enforcement because
the ship owners had given them $2 million in advertising. But
Redfield was intimidated; he allowed the Great Lakes excur-

sion steamer *Eastland,* threatened with bankruptcy, to ignore
the provision requiring lifeboats for all passengers. La Follette's
campaign to compel the Wilson administration to enforce the
law tragically succeeded on July 24, 1915, when the *Eastland,*
overflowing with 2500 sightseers, overturned in the Chicago
River, killing more than 1000 passengers. The "ship owners'
greed conspired with government complaisance," charged La
Follette.

Haunted by the vision of ship owner bankruptcy, Treasury
Secretary William G. McAdoo investigated the companies. In
October 1915 he issued a public letter condemning them as
liars. The Pacific Mail's stock had doubled in value since the
act's passage, he declared, and it had sold ships to make a $1
million profit, not because it could not afford to obey the act.
The Wilson administration then enforced the act more rigor-
ously. The seamen's "emancipation," like the railroad
workers' shorter hours, was achieved, in the end, not by a
consumer crusade for the traveling public, but by a producer-
oriented campaign to assist interest groups.

Although La Follette supported modernizers' campaigns to
help the corporations' victims, he remained too insurgent to
support Wilson's program for regulating business in 1914.
Believing that competition was the best process by which
consumers could obtain justice from corporations, La Follette
wanted government to help in the following ways: by automatically breaking up any corporation that controlled 30 per
cent of its market; by requiring corporations to pay repara-
tions to their victims when they used practices that undermined competition; by fixing personal guilt for monopolistic
practices by imprisoning corporate officials; and by denying
prosecutors broad discretionary powers by listing specific practices that were always criminal acts. But the Wilsonians, as in
their banking program, seemed to have defined their goal as
the promotion of economic growth through conciliation
among interest groups.

Wilson, La Follette believed, surrendered to pressure from

businessmen for self-regulation when in 1914 he championed a Federal Trade Commission in which government would advise corporations about vaguely-prohibited unfair practices and only rarely prosecute them. He was pleased, however, that the FTC would have broad powers to investigate and expose corporate wrongdoing, for he agreed with Brandeis, that "publicity . . . will go far toward preventing monopoly." Although he wanted to outlaw industrial holding companies, he cheered the act's prohibition of interlocking directorates.

La Follette believed that the true test of the best ways to regulate corporations would come in the oldest area of regulation, the one in which he had the longest experience, that of the railroads. In 1913 Congress enacted his proposal to establish railroad rates on the basis of actual investments in physical property because it was an objective way of allowing the railroads a reasonable profit. When in 1913 and 1914 special Interstate Commerce Commission investigators exposed the ways in which banking syndicates and speculators had looted railroads, La Follette proclaimed that the ICC should make no further rate decisions until it had completed its physical valuation and that the railroads should not expect consumers and shippers to subsidize their greed and incompetence in the form of high rates or poor service. Focusing now on internal management practices, La Follette assumed that honest and efficient managements would guarantee justice to consumers.

La Follette battled the Wilsonians sharply over three railroad policies in 1914. The first battle was initiated by the eastern railroads, who, pleading imminent bankruptcy, petitioned the ICC for a 5 per cent rate increase. In May, La Follette took 366 pages of the *Congressional Record* to expose their massive campaign among businessmen and journalists. He charged that they were poor because speculators had looted them. In July the ICC attacked the railroads' propaganda campaign, endorsed the Brandeis–La Follette argument that inefficiency and watered stock were the chief causes of financial problems, and denied the general rate increase.

The railroads then appealed directly to President Wilson's fear of a depression. Wilson publicly announced that "all fair assistance [should be] rendered ungrudgingly." On September 19, 1914, the ICC took the hint and reopened the case. This time, the railroads charged that their poverty resulted from harassment by insurgent politicians, state regulatory commissions, and the ICC; and this time the ICC granted the increase. In a slashing editorial, La Follette roasted the ICC for surrendering to the railroads and to Wilson at the expense of consumers, who would pay an additional $100 million for the increase.

The ICC reversal had been brought about by two of Wilson's 1914 appointees, Henry C. Hall and Winthrop M. Daniels, whose confirmation had been fought bitterly by La Follette. Daniels was perhaps the most conservative state regulator in the country; he believed that corporations were entitled to financial return, not only on their investment, but also on their good will. To win Daniels's confirmation, Wilson needed the support of conservative Republicans in order to compensate for the loss of Democrats who absented themselves rather than comply with the president's rigorous imposition of caucus discipline. In April 1914 Daniels was confirmed by a 36-to-27 vote; La Follette risked possible expulsion from the Senate by exposing in his magazine the vote, which had been taken in executive session. Charging that Wilson had betrayed progressives, La Follette declared that Daniels's appointment "reminds thoughtful men of the beginning of the second year of the reign of one William Howard Taft."

La Follette's next attack was on the administration's bill to regulate railroad securities. La Follette claimed that Wall Street wanted this bill to restore the shaky investor confidence in plummeting railroad stocks by giving them federal sanction. The government should not sanction the prices of securities, he said; prices should be determined by open-market competition. La Follette maintained that the Wilson administration wanted this scheme and the rate increase for a "rail-

road prosperity" that would keep it in power. La Follette
succeeded in killing the railroad security plan.

The events of 1914 convinced La Follette that regulation of
the railroads by independent commission would fail. On September 5, 1914, in his magazine he formally opened debate on
the question of whether government ownership was preferable
to ICC regulation. "Transportation must be made a servant of
the public, not a private instrument of financial power," he
announced in beginning the debate. He spent 1915 and 1916
collecting information on government-owned railroads in
Europe. He told Rudolph Spreckels and Charles Crane that he
would direct a public ownership movement if they would
finance a staff and publicity bureau for three years. Finally, in
December of 1916, he and John R. Commons prepared the last
details for the campaign. It was halted only by the intervention of the war and government management of the railroads
during the war.

The differences between La Follette and Wilson were clear.
Wilson and the Democrats identified people in terms of their
jobs, and they wanted corporations to ensure expanding prosperity for farmers, workers, and businessmen. Through the
FRB, FTC, and their railroad policies they created stable
mechanisms for predictable growth that would conciliate conflicting pressures from interest groups. La Follette, who
doubted that Americans identified with their jobs or that they
worshipped economic growth, wanted corporations to ensure
good, cheap, and safe services to consumers without robbing
the community of profit. He attacked the modernizers for their
failure to confront concentrated wealth and power, the root of
the problem. Competition, he believed, best ensured good
products and services at reasonable prices and profits. Government should ensure that the management practices of corporations benefitted consumers, and it should strip corporations of
special economic privileges (such as rebates) and political
privileges (such as sanctioning railroad securities) that retarded competition. Modernizers believed that private prop-

erty was essential for economic growth, but by 1916 La Follette, who demanded to know how property was used, had concluded that the railroads would only serve consumers if they became public property.

As the progressive movement shifted rapidly during Wilson's first term from insurgency toward modernization, many voters believed that it was betraying its origins as a democratic movement to help taxpayers. Charles McCarthy, in publicizing *The Wisconsin Idea* (1912), admitted that commission government ran "seemingly contrary to our idea of democracy," but insisted that the commissions could help people more efficiently than they could help themselves. Modernizing professionals rejected the nineteenth-century idea that the individual could control his own fate and the corollary that poverty, disease, and unemployment were products of individual weakness and failure. They argued that the individual was a product of his environment; they wanted to make new individuals by making new environments. By the 1910s, as professionals increasingly directed social amelioration, the question of who was to determine the ideal person to be created by manipulating the environment became a very live issue. Many professionals seemed to be assuming that they knew what was best for people and to be imposing programs upon them. This raised the people's old fear that someone was trying to force them to accept alien values.

Experts and their commissions seemed not only too remote from many consumers and too expensive for taxpayers, but also too often to be protecting the very businesses they were intended to regulate, as La Follette had charged against the ICC. The *Lincoln Daily Star* lamented in 1914 that Nebraska's railroad commission actually made regulation more difficult, because it joined with the railroads to resist reform pressure from the unorganized majority of voters. Alfred H. Smith, president of the New York Central railroad, eulogized commissions in 1914 because they protected railroads from radicals. As professional and scientific criteria for regulating business supplanted the original criterion of majority control, many voters who had supported insurgent progressivism rejected modernizing progressivism.

The disastrous election of 1914 in Wisconsin taught La Follette that conservatives could appeal to taxpayers and citizens as well as progressives could. Five progressive candidates entered the 1914 gubernatorial primary against corporate manager Emanuel Philipp. Conservatives charged that the "tax-eating commissions" that constituted the Wisconsin Idea formed an elitist, unresponsive "bureaucracy." In the name of democracy and lower taxes, the conservatives blasted the rising costs of state government. La Follette fully recognized this new taxpayers' revolt, agreeing with a Beloit lieutenant that "the taxation problem is by far the most serious thing that we have had to contend with for some time." He argued repeatedly in *La Follette's* that the commissions saved more than they cost, but he was privately angry at his lieutenants for raising state budgets so fast. Philipp won the primary, and John J. Blaine, La Follette's candidate for governor on an independent ticket in the general election, lost badly to Philipp. His heart "sad and heavy," La Follette lectured Wisconsin's voters from his magazine: Philipp's election "is a complete repudiation of the much heralded Wisconsin Idea."

La Follette saw that the Wisconsin result paralleled that of the nation, as conservatives condemned progressives for modernizing elitism that undermined popular government and for pandering to interest groups in the name of social amelioration. Progressives seemed no longer interested in the unorganized consumers and taxpayers. When progressives increasingly stopped their appeals to taxpayers, many conservative Republicans, like Philipp, saw a new popular base for their return to power. Rejected by voters between 1908 and 1912 when they had attacked government regulations as a handicap to businessmen, these conservatives now attacked government regulations because they cost taxpayers too much and only benefitted special interest groups. In 1914 Democrats lost 120 seats in the House, mostly to conservative Republicans.

As insurgency's emphasis on uniting people across class lines ebbed with the rising power of job-oriented groups, many voters returned to their ethnic and religious identifications. Cultural differences once again threatened the progressive movement. The 1914 elections split insurgent voters along religious lines in Wisconsin, as elsewhere. As rural evangelicals felt an economic necessity to organize on their own, reflected in the rapid growth of farm groups and cooperative marketing, they blamed their problems on cities and their Catholic populations. The economic recession of 1913–1914 and the outbreak of war in Europe heightened ethnic and religious competition. Furthermore, national insurgents had carried their programs so far from the immediate concerns of consumers and taxpayers that the Roman Church was about as meaningful an enemy as The System. The victim in Wisconsin was La Follette's choice for the Senate, Catholic Lieutenant Governor Tom Morris, who failed miserably among the rural, evangelical Scandinavians. La Follette was appalled, after a visit to Wisconsin, by the viciousness of the bigotry, unparalleled in his political experience. He told one voter who wanted to drive Catholics out of office: "If a majority of the people of Wisconsin [think] that some religious issue [is] paramount they must get that kind of statesman for Wisconsin. . . . I [am] not the man for it." The dramatic revival of ethno-religious conflict undermined insurgents' hopes for reuniting people as consumers, taxpayers, and citizens.

As cultural differences increasingly divided insurgents, La Follette discovered that differences over racial questions were at least as bitter as those over religion. As a congressman in the 1880s he had attacked southern whites for trying to deprive blacks of their voting rights and for trying to deny the North its victory in the Civil War. He was appalled in the

1910s when Democrats, with southern white constituents, tried to establish racial segregation within government departments.

La Follette hated segregation because it created artificial barriers, which retarded insurgency. After speaking tours of the South in 1913 and 1915, La Follette concluded that "there is more material to build [an insurgent movement on] in the colored race in the south than in the poor whites" because blacks had made much greater educational progress than poor whites and "in all of this struggle for real democracy the problem is to get the people to *understand*." La Follette might agree with Mississippi's James K. Vardaman on every other major issue, but Vardaman was such a vicious segregationist and racist that La Follette could never feel that they both belonged to the same movement. La Follette joined other insurgent Republicans in bitterly attacking Vardaman and other Democrats for excluding blacks from the benefits of federal aid to southern farmers in the Smith-Lever Act of 1914. La Follette agreed with the only southern insurgent he ever understood, Chief Justice Walter Clark of the North Carolina Supreme Court: "The South . . . is by no means progressive and owing no doubt to our peculiar institutions, never has been."

Belle shared Robert's determination to fight segregation despite the pressures against such a fight from many southern voters and magazine readers who, like Vardaman, agreed with them on most other issues. Belle lectured early in 1914 to predominantly black audiences in Washington and New York on the evils of segregation. Together they decided to risk the rebellion of southern subscribers by using *La Follette's* to expose the Wilsonians' segregation policy in 1913 and 1914. In one article, Belle described three veteran black women employees of the Bureau of Printing and Engraving who were suddenly told that they had to eat their lunches at a separate table. The fledgling National Association for the Advancement of Colored People fed some of its information to *La Follette's* for widespread exposure.

La Follette was afraid in 1914 that his beloved magazine would also be a casualty of the collapse of insurgency. Circulation had stabilized at a point just under 40,000 readers, not nearly enough to pay the magazine's debts. With the movement clearly declining, wealthy benefactors were no longer willing to bail it out. In July 1914 Spreckels said that his $3500 contribution would be his last to the magazine. Believing that the magazine was a crucial vehicle for vindicating his record, La Follette rejected Brandeis's advice to kill it. In late 1914 he changed it from a weekly to a monthly. By April 1915 he was again describing it as "the rat hole" that deprived him of financial security, and he appealed to subscribers for donations. *La Follette's* continued on this basis for the rest of its publisher's life.

Although the movement that had rewarded La Follette's driving need for a record was rapidly ebbing, that need continued. He collapsed again from nervous exhaustion in the summer of 1914 and did not attend the Senate again until late that year. He then began to devote more of his energy to teaching his son Robert the same need.

Robert, Jr., however, early in 1915 discovered a way to stop his father from constantly imposing his own demonic zeal for work and even win his father's support. He contacted a streptococcic infection that he could not shake, suffering relapses that were sometimes critical and lasted for most of the year. Senator La Follette, on a speaking tour, wrote his son that he was finally passing his father's character test, that his battle with the infection was "the biggest and bravest and hardest thing of your whole life." The same drama was reenacted in 1918 and 1919 when Robert Jr. again battled an infection that left him often near death and paralyzed for a time. This time Belle took her son to La Jolla, California, to recuperate far from her husband's pressures, and Robert Jr. did not rejoin his father for another year.

Belle reminded La Follette that during the 1915 and 1918 illnesses they had discussed how "this idea that he had not met his responsibility, had not made the most of his power and opportunity — had preyed upon [their son]." She urged La Follette to relax his pressure. But La Follette could not, for he had determined that his son would carry on his work. He wrote Robert Jr. in 1919, "When the last night comes and I go to the Land of Never Return — what an awful account of *things undone* I shall leave behind. . . . A week is really a lot of time out of the short end of life — when every tick of the clock seems to say 'hurry,' 'hurry.' " La Follette hoped that his son at least would understand the passions for work and a clean record that drove him so relentlessly.

After the disastrous results in 1914, La Follette felt determined to win the voters' approval in his reelection campaign of 1916. Governor Philipp and the conservatives had so effectively harnessed the taxpayers' revolt that he needed a massive speaking campaign to reeducate the voters. In September 1915 he went to Madison to prepare for those speeches. He wanted to convince Wisconsin voters that progressive government had improved their daily lives. "I never worked harder," he wrote Belle after putting in sixteen-hour-days to collect facts to vindicate his and the progressives' record. He had to prove that progressives had saved the voters from the old system of "indirect taxes from high freight rates, high gas and electric rates, high insurance rates, and the escape of all corporations from taxation." He would again be the teacher, convincing voters that they felt powerless not because of high taxes and remote commissions but because a few big businessmen controlled their destinies. Experts were needed to fight the power of the business elite.

In November he finally felt "the confidence of thorough preparation" and began the campaign. He spoke in Wisconsin whenever he could escape from the Senate over the next five months. "I am feeling good," he told Belle, "and am making good speeches and bringing the old fellows back into line." He soon discovered that the war in Europe was troubling voters more than state issues, and he modified his position, telling voters that the corporations that had oppressed them at home were now trying to destroy American democracy by militarizing it and taking the country to war. He won the election for delegates to the Republican National Convention with 110,064 votes for his slate to 70,813 for Philipp's.

La Follette had an easy campaign for renomination to the Senate because he was fighting a conservative warhawk, M. G. Jeffris. Jeffris charged that La Follette was too sympathetic toward Germany, but, unfortunately for Jeffris, hostility toward Germany ebbed rapidly in April 1916, when that country ended its submarine campaign. Wilson himself had felt the rapid change in mood. He had hoped the Democratic convention would kindle support for Americanism and military spending, but the Democratic delegates went wild instead for the keynote speech by Martin H. Glynn, former New York governor, when he argued that neutrality, not preparedness, was America's heritage. Out of the convention came a very different theme than Wilson had intended: "He kept us out of war." La Follette picked it up, arguing that corporations were trying to force the country into war.

La Follette easily won renomination, but he failed to carry his gubernatorial candidate, William Hatton, to victory against Philipp. Philipp had significantly cut state taxes, but, more important, he, like La Follette, appealed to the individual's desire to discipline remote governments that dictated taxes or war to them. Hatton, like La Follette's opponent Jeffris, had championed schemes that would cost more taxes and produce more regimentation over individuals' lives. In fact, La Follette was less embarrassed by Philipp's presence on the ticket than he was by that of presidential candidate Charles Evans Hughes, a reputed progressive who attacked the

Seamen's Act and the railroad hours law. Wisconsin's voters seemed to share his feelings about the ticket, for on the eve of American entrance into World War I, Wisconsin voters gave a split verdict on progressivism. La Follette led the Republican ticket to victory in November, winning the Senate with 65 per cent of the vote, while Philipp carried the governorship with 58 per cent and Hughes carried Wisconsin with 53 per cent.

La Follette himself was never more popular. Farmers and workers who had come to identify with their jobs appreciated his support of rural credits and relief for railroad workers, seamen, and organized labor generally. Other voters clearly retained their ethno-religious identities, strengthened by war in Europe, and many of them continued to think like taxpayer insurgents, protesting against a government they could not control. This led them to simultaneous support for La Follette, now reputed to be one of the nation's foremost radicals, and Philipp, a forerunner of modern conservatives who would harness taxpayer consciousness into an attack on big government.

The 1916 election in Wisconsin revealed that the old ideological battles that had split the party were ebbing in favor of loyalty to party. La Follette and Philipp did best in the same areas that had supported both Taft and Roosevelt in 1912, and La Follette and Phillipp received their strongest support from the same areas. La Follette continued to run best in rural Scandinavian areas, but he gained more votes among Germans and in cities. His growing support for labor unions, his indifference to morals issues, and his championship of neutrality made him attractive to his new supporters.

The great lesson of the 1916 election was that foreign policy had become the burning issue among voters. The spontaneous demonstration that had disrupted the plans of Wilson's managers in 1916 and voter support that relieved La Follette of the need to hinge his reelection on a defense of expensive commissions, this yearning for peace, remained the basic grass-roots feeling.

VII

Insurgency in
a Revolutionary World
1917–1919

THE SUDDEN OUTBREAK of war and revolution throughout the world deepened the gulf between Wilson and La Follette. By 1917, the senator had become the leading critic of Democratic foreign policy, and by his opposition to the war he regained the position of national leadership he had lost in 1912. Insurgents and modernizers had cooperated on many domestic issues during Wilson's first term, but the war strengthened the conservative drift in Wilson and among modernizers generally, opening an enormous chasm between the two ideologies and leaders.

La Follette's position on foreign policy, like that of other insurgents, had evolved gradually. Preoccupied with his campaigns against the domestic power of large corporations, he had largely ignored foreign policy in the first decade of the twentieth century and had endorsed his party's positions in a desultory way. He agreed with Republican leaders that foreign markets were necessary for the products of American farms and factories. As an insurgent leader, however, he soon began to understand that other peoples, like Americans, were struggling to control their own lives. He defended the abortive 1905 revolution in Russia and, unlike most Republicans, voted for Philippine independence in 1907.

By 1910 or 1911, La Follette had begun to see American foreign policy as an instrument of big business, as a further example of how corporations subverted popular rule. The outbreak of social revolution in Mexico was the cause that crystallized his belief. When, in 1911, Taft and other conservative Republicans suggested that the United States might intervene in Mexico to protect American property, La Follette charged that the cry for intervention stemmed from businessmen who feared that their investments, secured under the corrupt dictatorship of the recently-deposed Porfirio Diaz, would be threatened by the revolutionaries. La Follette and the insurgents identified completely with the Mexican *insurrectos*. By 1916, La Follette had broadened his analysis of the Mexican experience into an insurgent critique that linked corporate exploitation at home and abroad: "Privilege exploits us folks here in our own United States [and] makes so much money out of us that it creates a huge surplus. Privilege, never satiated, wants this surplus to be at work bringing in still more profits. Weak and undeveloped (and unexploited!) countries offer the biggest returns."

The same corporations that exploited consumers and workers at home thus created the pressures for an expansionist foreign policy. War, imperialism, military spending, all were new forms of what La Follette had once called the supreme issue: "The encroachment of the powerful few upon the rights of the many."

At first the election of Woodrow Wilson had seemed to promise a shift away from the policies of Roosevelt and Taft. The new president had promised that he would substitute honor for the dollars and bullets that his predecessors had used. But Wilson, like his predecessors, believed that the United States ought to play a large role in world politics. In Mexico he preferred elections and arbitration among contending groups to the country's condition of revolution and bloodshed, and he repeatedly tried to persuade the Mexicans — even with American military interventions in 1914 and

1916 – to accept such modernizing and accommodating institutions. Indeed, within a few years the Wilson administration had intervened in the affairs of Latin American countries to a degree unprecedented during the administrations of Roosevelt and Taft. Wilson never understood that some peoples might find revolution necessary to achieve self-government, for to him self-government was achieved as soon as modernizing institutions like free elections in Mexico (or the Federal Trade Commission in the United States) were established. He had to intervene in other countries often to persuade them of this truth that many seemed strangely to doubt.

La Follette bitterly opposed American interventions in Mexico in 1914 and 1916. Such policies provoked sharp attacks from him and other insurgents who increasingly resisted American economic and military involvement in Latin America and the world. They opposed United States protectorates in Haiti and the Dominican Republic, blocked the inclusion in a treaty with Nicaragua of a provision that would have given the United States the right to intervene in that country's internal affairs, and vigorously supported independence for the Philippines. They believed that the best way to assist fellow insurgents throughout the world was to prevent American businessmen from launching invasions to recover their investments.

Once war broke out in Europe in 1914, moreover, Wilson moved steadily, if reluctantly, toward intervention, identifying American economic, strategic, and cultural interests with a victory by the French and British and holding the Germans to a "strict accountability" for destruction of American shipping. La Follette praised Wilson's initial proclamation calling for "strict neutrality," and he warmly supported the president's rejection of pressures from conservative Republicans that the United States embark on a program of expensive military preparations. In his magazine he exposed the "War Trust," charging that investment bankers, corporations, and their conservative Republican allies were promoting a campaign to arm

America in the name of preparedness and patriotism. The only way to prevent war, he declared in 1915, was to "take the profit out of war." On February 8, 1915, he introduced the La Follette Peace Resolution to bring the moral weight of neutral nations, led by the United States, to end the war. The resolution envisioned a conference of neutral nations to limit armaments and prohibit their export, establish an international tribunal, and require government ownership of munitions manufacture. Although some newspapers applauded the resolution, Wilson, who preferred informal means of seeking peace, blocked it in the Foreign Relations Committee.

As Wilson's position toward Germany began to harden, and as he began to call for military preparedness, La Follette launched his opposition to the president that would lead him ultimately to become a new hero to millions of Americans. Wilson saw that trade with the European belligerents was not only pulling the American economy out of a depression but promoting faster economic growth than the country had experienced in a long time. Fearing a crash, the president reversed himself and allowed American investment bankers to lend billions of dollars to the allies to buy American goods, thus generating more jobs for workers and markets for farmers and businessmen. When Germany resorted to submarines early in 1915 to break the British blockade against American goods, Wilson made the fateful decision to hold Germany accountable for American deaths from the submarines while, in effect, allowing the British to intercept American goods headed toward the continent. Wilson's trade policy was a dramatic expression of modernization's job-oriented emphasis upon economic growth at home.

La Follette felt, in turns, furious and desperate as he observed that policy through an insurgent's eyes. The price of the war boom at home was crippling inflation for consumers, skyrocketing taxes, unprecedented profits, and the probable entrance of the United States into the war. The price of wheat doubled within a year after the war broke out, pleasing Wilson's job-oriented farmers but infuriating La Follette's consumers. Prices rose so rapidly in 1916 and early 1917, La Follette declared, that "the problem of mere existence overshadows all other problems." Nationwide boycotts of food products whose prices had skyrocketed in 1915–1916 gave way to full-scale food riots in many cities in early 1917. In the months before American entrance into the war, La Follette was reminded of the French Revolution by scenes of "hungry mothers with hungry babes in their arms and hungry children at their heels . . . surging through the streets of our largest cities screaming vainly for bread." La Follette blamed this problem on the unprecedented profits that resulted from the war trade. U.S. Steel's profits fell from $81 million in 1913 to $24 million in 1914, but, when the war boom began, its profits leaped to $76 million in 1915 and $272 million in 1916. The Armour meat-packing corporation trebled its profits from 1914 to 1916. More than one-third of all millionaires living in the United States in 1916 had become millionaires that very year as a result of the war boom.

If the war boom enriched corporations at the consumers' expense, La Follette argued, the preparedness campaign, which Wilson reversed himself to support late in 1915, enriched the largest corporations, particularly the munitions makers, at the taxpayers' expense. With Wilson's support in 1916, preparedness advocates doubled the 1915 military appropriation. Government munitions contracts, while helping workers and businessmen, constituted the ultimate robbery of taxpayers by privileged corporations. The real danger was not lack of preparedness, wrote La Follette in 1916, but "the tide of sentiment that, under the guise of patriotism, is actually based on commercial greed."

Worse, La Follette argued, Wilson's policy was not neutral; it supported the Allies. By September 1915 he believed that the need to maintain prosperity by supporting corporate investments in the Allied cause, investments that would be lost if the Germans won the war, determined Wilson's policy. The United States was "underwriting the success of the cause of the Allies."

La Follette tried frantically to reverse the policy. He nearly accepted Henry Ford's invitation to sail on Ford's Peace Ship, which he regarded as "one of the biggest pieces of work in the history of mankind." He did accept Ford's donation to pay for the distribution of 150,000 copies of his major speech attacking Wilson's "neutrality" policy. Finally, in 1916, a desperate La Follette concluded that if war was a result of the trade policy that produced prosperity, then he favored peace and depression. He demanded a neutral policy like Jefferson's during the Napoleonic wars, when the government embargoed all trade with belligerents and caused a depression at home. When La Follette renounced all trade at whatever economic cost to Americans, he showed how deeply his insurgency ran counter to job-oriented modernization.

The insurgents believed that the majority supported them despite the superficial patriotism of newspapers, motion pictures, and preparedness parades. By early 1917 La Follette assumed that "leading newspapers have been retained by the interests and are now being actually subsidized to force on the war." Since insurgency depended heavily on exposure, "the defection of the daily press has been a staggering blow to democracy," declared Edward A. Ross. Insurgents suffered even more from recent corporation control over popular magazines, which, La Follette charged, allowed journalists to write only about "Spots on the Moon." La Follette believed the parades hardly revealed popular support for the war because they resulted in few recruits to the armed forces.

Convinced of majority support but finding the mass media increasingly hostile to their views, insurgents groped desperately for ways to mobilize mass support behind their resistance to a neutrality policy they feared would drag America into the war. William Jennings Bryan, who resigned as secretary of state in 1915 to protest Wilson's policy because it was too pro-

British and because it would lead the United States to war, launched a public speaking campaign for peace. La Follette applied the principle of direct democracy to foreign policy. On April 29, 1916, he introduced a bill that would establish an advisory referendum before the country could declare war. The people, "not the handful of men in positions of power," should decide. Insurgent Republicans like Norris and Clapp joined Hearst's *New York American* in welcoming La Follette's bill. When war seemed inevitable early in 1917, La Follette and Bryan worked feverishly to get congressional approval for the referendum.

Because the Wilson administration blocked the insurgents' proposal for a referendum on the war, the evidence on public reaction remains fragmentary. But much of the evidence which does exist suggests that La Follette and Bryan may have been correct. Many Americans, quite probably a majority, might have voted against the preparedness campaign and ultimately the declaration of war if the insurgents had succeeded in making foreign policy responsive to a popular vote. Indeed, warhawks never challenged the insurgents' claim that a majority opposed the war. Insurgents cited the results of head counts. A member of the Seattle School Board polled shoppers and found 31 in favor of the war and 374 opposed. Minnesota Congressman Ernest Lundeen polled his constituents and reported about 800 in favor and 8000 against. A mail ballot of 20,000 Massachusetts residents resulted in a two-thirds majority against the war. Official referenda managed by local election officials and held on election days in New Ulm, Minnesota, recorded 19 in favor, 485 opposed, and in St. Peter, Minnesota, 26 for the war, 263 against, while in La Follette's Wisconsin, Yankee and Swiss Monroe voted 95 for the war declaration, 954 against, and German Sheboygan County tallied 6133 against the war, 17 in favor. Congressman William E. Mason of Illinois explained that he ignored organized pressure groups: "I am against this war because I know that people in my State are not for it. I am not quoting newspapers. I asked the people to write me; . . . and out of a thousand letters or telegrams, not exceeding five or ten have come asking for a declaration of war, and those as a rule can be traced to gentlemen interested in war as a business."

Prowar modernizers insisted that the people spoke through organized political and economic elites. Senator Atlee Pomerene of Ohio used support from the Chambers of Commerce of Newark, Columbus, and Youngstown, from the Harvard Club of Ohio, and the Ohio State Automobile Association to show that Ohio favored the war. The accuracy of reports from mass meetings, cited by prowar senators, is doubtful. Mayor J. E. Chase of Jacksonville, Florida, organized a meeting of 1800 of the city's "best citizens" which unanimously supported the war, reported the *Jacksonville Times-Union*. But a painter counted only 469 people at the meeting and reported that at least half did not vote on the war issue because they feared reprisals from the city's elite if they publicly expressed their antiwar feelings.

The overwhelming prowar vote in Congress only showed that modernizers dominated the political process. Job-oriented interest groups, particularly businessmen, would promote the maintenance of economic growth even if it meant war. Indifferent to consumers and taxpayers, they rolled over the insurgents into preparedness and war. Left behind were those who charged that the war was caused, if not by special interests, then by the materialism that accompanied the worship of economic growth. George Norris angrily declared that "we are about to put the dollar sign upon the American flag."

Although Congress did not vote war until April 1917, the crowded weeks preceeding that vote witnessed the same conflict between the administration's insistence on the right to trade and economic growth and the insurgents' demand that the people be allowed to vote. When Germany resumed its submarine campaign early in 1917, American ship owners and shippers refused to send their cargoes into the war zone without armed protection from the government. On February 26,

Wilson bowed to their pressure and asked Congress for authority to arm merchant ships. Leaking an intercepted note by the German Foreign Secretary that seemed to prove Germany's warlike intentions toward the United States, he demanded that Congress act before it adjourned for nine months on March 4.

Since the armed-ship bill reached the Senate floor with only 49 hours remaining in the session, La Follette organized a filibuster that would give voters time to restrain the rush toward war. After debating the bill on March 2, the Senate met at 10:00 A.M. on March 3 for a continuous 26-hour session that would end in adjournment at noon on the fourth. During the afternoon and night, insurgents punctuated their filibuster with frantic conferences and brief naps. The tension mounted as the morning dawned. The Wilsonians circulated a petition, signed by 76 senators, that demanded an end to the filibuster. La Follette knew that he would receive the worst abuse because he would speak last. As his aides piled his desk with documents from which he planned to read, Works and Clapp aided the filibuster in their last Senate speeches. When La Follette arrived to begin his speech, he learned that his name had been removed from the list of speakers.

Anger was turning to rumors of violence as the majority wanted to vote on the bill or at least to prevent La Follette, the filibusterers' ringleader, from speaking. La Follette glanced down at his travelling bag in which he kept a gun to protect himself in lonely railroad stations, not knowing that his son had removed the gun because he feared his father might shoot someone. When Norris finished at 9:30 A.M. on March 4, the presiding officer recognized Owen. Before Owen finished, La Follette was on his feet screaming for recognition, but the presiding officer recognized Gilbert Hitchcock, the bill's floor manager. La Follette stood in the center aisle demanding the floor. Democrats, led by Kentucky's Ollie James, swarmed and rushed toward La Follette, and Oregon's Harry Lane spotted a gun under James' coat. Lane fingered his rattail file and moved toward La Follette, determined to stab James if he reached for his gun. La Follette bellowed: "I will continue on this floor until I complete my statement unless somebody carries me off, and I should like to see the man who will do it." The Senate voted 52 to 12 to require La Follette to sit down. Rage trembling through his body, La Follette repeatedly objected to Hitchcock's unanimous consent requests that the Senate agree to vote on the bill that day. Although Hitchcock and the Democrats prevented La Follette from making the speech he wanted to answer what he knew would be torrents of abuse, La Follette succeeded in blocking the bill's passage. Belle called the filibuster that La Follette had organized "the greatest service it has ever come to you to render."

Wilson led the reaction that fell upon La Follette and the ten other filibusterers. Wilson told the press: "A little group of willful men, representing no opinion but their own, have rendered the great Government of the United States helpless and contemptible." "Von La Follette" took his orders from the Kaiser, charged the *Cincinnati Post*.

On March 9, Wilson announced that he would ignore Congress and arm merchant ships by executive order. Now the merchants could trade again, and the ships that carried America's domestic prosperity in their holds, ventured into the war zone. Nine days later German submarines sank three American ships. Wilson would wait no longer; everyone knew that he wanted a declaration of war when he addressed Congress on April 2.

Proclaiming that "the world must be made safe for democracy," Wilson asked for the war declaration. La Follette predicted a ten-to-one vote against the declaration if the Senate would enact his war referendum. "The poor, sir, who are the ones called upon to rot in the trenches, have no organized power," he warned the Senate, "but oh, Mr. President, at some time they will be heard." After asking why a war to save democracy was to be declared without a popular vote, he concluded that Jefferson's neutrality policy was the only one that could have prevented the war. John Sharp Williams of Mississippi promptly concluded that La Follette was a better German than the German leaders. Finally, as midnight approached on April 4, the Senate voted 82 to 6 for the war, with Republicans Gronna and Norris and Democrats Lane, Stone, and Vardaman joining La Follette. Editors stepped up their attacks on the "traitor La Follette." The *Boston Evening Transcript* charged that La Follette's opposition to the war was "the disloyal culmination of a career of selfish Ishmaelitism. . . . Standing against his own country and for his country's enemies, he is gone and fallen. . . . Henceforth he is the Man without a Country."

American participation in the war intensified the conservative and increasingly repressive character of the Wilson administration, which now sought to rally the country behind the war and suppress popular opposition. La Follette drew around him the antiwar progressives from both parties and mounted attacks on the draft, on the administration's tax policies, and on the destruction of civil liberties, and by so doing became once again an idol to millions.

The declaration of war inaugurated a battle over the meaning of democracy and sacrifice in wartime. The first job was to recruit the men to fight. The groups that favored the war wanted a draft instead of seeking volunteers. Business and professional men vigorously promoted conscription. Major business organizations petitioned Congress from New York, Philadelphia, Boston, Cincinnati, and from towns from Massachusetts to North Carolina and Montana to Texas. They were joined in support of the draft by specialized business groups like the Employers Association of the Inland Empire at Spokane, the Western Pine Manufacturers Association, the Automobile Club of America, the Montana Stock Growers Association, the American Merchants Syndicate, and the California State Realty Federation, as well as engineering societies, bar associations, and newspaper groups.

La Follette and the antiwar insurgents believed that the

prowar forces had conceded the unpopularity of the war when they rejected the insurgents' preference for recruiting an army from volunteers who supported the war, and they believed that the howl of the corporate elite for the draft proved something even more sinister. "They would take the youth of the land while it is yet impressionable," cried Congressman George Huddleston of Alabama, "force it into their armies, rob it of its principles of democracy, teach it docility and respect for them and their property, so that the New World might be made over to resemble the Old, with its castes of prestige and privilege." The draft, argued La Follette, gave the corporations the power to turn independent young men into "mere automatons." "Every interest, every newspaper, every man who has been opposing popular government in this country" was united to compel conscription, he said. La Follette proposed unsuccessful amendments that broadened the exemption for conscientious objectors and that required a referendum before conscription could go into effect. Citing the overwhelming rejection of conscription in a 1916 referendum in Australia, La Follette observed: "Never in all my many years of experience in the House and in the Senate have I heard so much democracy preached and so little practiced as during the last few months." The Senate adopted conscription by a 65-to-8 vote.

La Follette was deeply disturbed by the Wilson administration's Espionage Act to suppress freedom of speech, assembly, and the press in wartime. Newspapers organized a campaign that successfully blocked Wilson's demand for a presidential censorship board by one vote in the Senate, but no other group was powerful enough to defeat the act's other repressive provisions. As a magazine publisher, La Follette was particularly angered by the section authorizing the Post Office to deny mailing privileges to publications. In the end, only five other senators joined him in voting against the Espionage Act.

The debate over the bill to apportion the war's staggering costs divided Americans along job-oriented lines. The

Trenton Chamber of Commerce favored issuing bonds to be repaid in the future instead of taxing incomes and profits because income and profit taxes were "detrimental to the prosperity of the land" and would discourage "the productive capacity of our people." One corporation after another echoed the Trenton Chamber, including the Kentucky Manufacturers and Shippers Association, the Atlanta Merchants and Manufacturers Association, the National Piano Manufacturers Association, and dozens of individual corporations. Workers and farmers were equally eager to soak the rich who had caused the war. The North Dakota State Federation of Labor, the Farmers National Committee, and the Boise Trade and Labor Council were joined in their petitions by local unions from Illinois, New York, Connecticut, Michigan, Massachusetts, and Wisconsin.

La Follette believed that the war tax issue would unite the antiwar forces and rekindle insurgency. He submitted a minority report to the Finance Committee's bill that shifted the burden from loans and consumption taxes to "surplus" incomes and "war" profits. He realized that in doing so he was no longer appealing to taxpayers recruited from all classes, but frankly to poor workers and farmers. The tax issue created "a sharp conflict of interest . . . between the different classes of our people."

From July through September 1917 he pressed his campaign. Arguing that coffee, tea, sugar, medicines, railroad travel, and telephone calls were "largely articles the consumption of which is necessary to maintain the health and well-being of the mass of people," La Follette tried to persuade the Senate to remove taxes on consumption. Saying, "It would be a reproach to our present civilization if we failed to prevent, so far as we have the power through taxation, one class of our citizens, comparatively small, from becoming enormously rich out of this war, while the other and much larger class was impoverished by the war," he suggested that individuals and corporations who profited from the war should return to their government every penny in excess of their prewar incomes and profits. Why should the United States tax war profits at an average rate of 31 per cent when Britain taxed war profits at 80 per cent?

Wilsonians completed their alliance with conservative Republicans as they answered La Follette's charges. Corporations produced economic growth, claimed Wilsonian leader Furnifold M. Simmons of North Carolina. To tax the rich would be "killing the goose that lays the golden egg [at a time when] everything must be done to stimulate productivity." Republican Porter J. McCumber of North Dakota feared that to tax the rich would "dampen their ardor and destroy their war spirit."

La Follette won widespread public support but only minor victories in the Senate. The Senate halved the bill's proposed consumption taxes, removing taxes on tea, coffee, cocoa, sugar, and postage. When La Follette tried to increase the amount raised by "surplus" income taxes from the bill's $417 million to $850 million, the Senate added another $64 million to the income tax section. The Senate added nearly one-half billion dollars to the amount to be raised from war-profits taxes on corporations.

La Follette clearly reemerged as the leader of an insurgent bloc that would have completely overhauled the bill to soak the rich. Unlike the insurgent bloc in the Taft years, the wartime group crossed party lines. It included Republicans Borah, Gronna, Kenyon, Norris, Hiram Johnson, Wesley Jones of Washington, sometimes Poindexter and Cummins, and Democrats Reed, Kirby, Vardaman, Gore, Hardwick, and Husting. But the insurgent bloc was not the only one that included members of both parties. La Follette's amendments failed because the Wilsonian leaders, including Simmons, Overman, Hitchcock, Newlands, and Hoke Smith, made common cause with conservative Republicans like Brandegee, Kellogg, Lodge, Penrose, and Smoot.

The wartime struggle between insurgents and modernizers was becoming increasingly rooted, as in the tax fight, in class

differences. As taxpayers had supported the insurgents' revenue battle in their job-oriented capacities as farmers and
workers, so consumers supported the fight against wartime
inflation in their job-oriented organizations. Food prices skyrocketed, often doubling, in the first half of 1917. Dozens of
central labor bodies and local unions joined state federations
from Kansas and North Dakota in demanding relief. They
concluded, with a Chicago grand jury, that speculation and
profiteering by middlemen caused the soaring prices and had
to be curbed. But the Wilsonians were more interested in
rapid production of food for the war than in the plight of
consumers, and their Food Administration revealed how the
war vastly accelerated modernization. To obtain rapid production and reasonable profits to all parts of the food industry, the Food Administration encouraged formation of and
cooperation among job-oriented groups, established minimum
prices to farmers, sponsored self-regulation by commodity
exchanges, and abrogated antitrust laws that benefitted consumers. Consumers could do their part for the war by eating
less.

Modernization also appealed to a religious group — the
evangelicals — by incorporating one of the deepest evangelical
crusades — prohibition. The evangelicals secured prohibition
because they emphasized production-oriented arguments:
liquor wasted grains needed to feed the troops; saloons retarded the efficient mobilization of men and goods. Insurgents
like La Follette and Hiram Johnson continued to dodge prohibition. "Damn the liquor question, anyway," complained
Johnson privately. La Follette tried to escape the issue by
announcing his personal opposition to prohibition and then
voting for the constitutional amendment with the argument
that the states would only have an opportunity to consider
prohibition if Congress first adopted it.

The food and liquor issues typified the larger crisis for
patriotism and citizenship in the war. Job-oriented groups
were fragmented and could only become a majority by devel-

oping a patriotism that emphasized economic growth, their major common bond. Many employers and conservatives wanted to use the loyalty issue to suppress their prewar enemies and created semiofficial groups to intimidate workers, insurgents, and socialists behind a superpatriotic smokescreen. Under the guise of patriotism, two copper-mining companies spearheaded a vigilante group that herded 1186 striking copper workers in Bisbee, Arizona, into cattle cars on July 12, 1917, and shipped them off to the New Mexico desert to shift for themselves. Charging that the Nonpartisan League of wheat farmers in the Dakotas and Minnesota was composed of "red Socialists," corporate-dominated state and local officials arrested the league's leaders and banned its meetings.

The pattern of official suppression, newspaper demands for loyalty, and vigilante terror set the stage for La Follette to consolidate his position as a national leader of those who opposed the war and had long resisted corporate control. La Follette decided to rally the antiwar forces at the Nonpartisan League's convention in St. Paul on September 20, 1917. The league was trying to create a farmer-labor alliance to tax the rich and establish government ownership of basic industries. The auditorium was jammed when he arrived, and ten thousand more people waited in the streets. As he entered, the audience rose and roared a five-minute ovation. He never lost them as he traced the long struggle for liberation from corporate domination, described his tax plan to soak the rich, and reviewed his opposition to the war. "We know it, Bob!" they shouted. He digressed to describe the causes of the war. "I don't mean to say that we hadn't suffered grievances; we had — at the hands of Germany." The grievance was our right to carry munitions to England without being torpedoed by a submarine. The audience cheered. When a heckler asked about the *Lusitania,* La Follette explained that Wilson never should have allowed the *Lusitania* to sail because he knew that it carried munitions. More cheers. La Follette was vindicating his record. It was 1907 again, and he was projecting his leadership of a movement that corporations and politicians wanted to suppress. As he and Belle returned to Madison that night, they were tremendously heartened by the warm reception from plain farmers and workers that contrasted so starkly, as it had ten years earlier, to the abuse he received in Washington.

The next morning La Follette became the main focus of official and vigilante campaigns to suppress antiwar spokesmen. The Associated Press reported that La Follette had said that the United States had *no* grievances against Germany and that the crowd had approved La Follette's disloyal defense of the sinking of the *Lusitania*. President Nicholas Murray Butler of Columbia University told an enthusiastic audience of the American Bankers Association that "you might just as well put poison in the food of every American boy that goes to his transport as to permit La Follette to talk as he does." *Staple's World* showed that the fear of revolt at home, not of treason, motivated these attacks when it lumped La Follette with the militant Industrial Workers of the World: "Far more capable, this man, than any I.W.W. . . . The poison of morbid unrest has fed the maggots of disorder and revolt. It is a shame to America, a shame to Wisconsin, that the Senate . . . must harbor a defender of the child-murderers who sank the *Lusitania*." The Minnesota Public Safety Commission petitioned the Senate to expel La Follette. Governor Joseph Burnquist announced that Minnesota was considering arresting La Follette under the Espionage Act. On September 29 the Senate referred the Minnesota petition for expulsion to the Committee on Privileges and Elections. "The war traders are making a campaign of it and the old tory crowd think it a good opportunity," La Follette telegraphed Belle.

The Senate galleries were jammed on October 6 because La Follette was scheduled to reply. La Follette tied his cause to that of the millions of less prominent Americans whose right to free speech was being abolished. After referring to a judge in Houston who wanted him shot by a firing squad, La Follette quoted another judge in North Dakota: "The Kaisers of high finance, who have been developing hatred of you for a generation because you have fought against them and for the common good, see this opportunity to turn the war patriotism into an engine of attack." La Follette charged that obscure citizens, lacking the forum given a senator, "are being terrorized and outraged in their rights by those sworn to uphold the laws and protect the rights of the people." "The most important question in this country to-day" was the right of citizens to discuss freely the issues of the war, for the voters "may be wiser than their leaders." After reviewing statements by English and American statesmen supporting free speech and the related right of Congress to specify American war aims, La Follette repeated that the majority opposed the war. When he finished, the galleries thundered loud applause; the vice-president had to gavel them into silence. Robert, Jr., listening from the gallery, believed that La Follette's speech "will do the hearts of the people good and will give them new hope for a return to the rights and freedoms guaranteed by our Constitution." Belle considered it her husband's finest speech.

Frank Kellogg of Minnesota, Joseph Robinson of Arkansas, and Albert Fall of New Mexico replied. Robinson said that La Follette belonged either in jail or in Germany. Fall best reflected the fears of La Follette's critics: "There is to-day a practical revolution going on in various parts of the country . . . and . . . utterances which might be perfectly proper at one time . . . are not proper at the present time." But the galleries were still with La Follette.

Official suppression and vigilante mobs had, La Follette believed, created an enormous antiwar feeling that was highly insurgent in its attitudes toward power and wealth, even though the people were bound together more by their sense of powerlessness as members of a class than as consumers. From politicians, farm leaders, journalists, and others he began collecting names of ordinary Americans opposed to the war to bombard with copies of the speech as preparation for an underground antiwar movement that would become public in time for the 1918 elections. Confronted by hostile elites on all sides, antiwar progressives finally forgot the old jealousies that had divided them since 1912, for, as La Follette wrote Gilson Gardner, a man whose admiration for Roosevelt had led to bitterness with La Follette since 1912, "Let's close the old books and open a new set. It's a time when friends of democracy should work together to save as much of the wreckage as possible." The antiwar socialists turned to La Follette when the government denied them use of the mails. In July 1917, Seymour Stedman turned over the subscriber list of the *Chicago Socialist* to La Follette saying that their prewar differences were irrelevant now. Eugene Debs wrote that La Follette's free speech address had already become a "classic" and that "if the plutocratic profiteers, the most shameless robbers in history, are 'patriots' under their own regime then you can well afford to be branded a 'traitor' and be proud of it." Leaders of the Nonpartisan League helped the campaign. Government suppression of meetings and publications of the Germans and Irish bonded them to the free speech movement. Insurgent congressmen and senators like Borah, Norris, Johnson, Gronna, Vardaman, Hollis, and Reed helped by championing free speech and exposing war profiteering.

La Follette and other antiwar leaders denounced the lack of free speech and assembly. When Herbert S. Bigelow, an old-time insurgent pastor in Cincinnati, was kidnapped and whipped, La Follette publicly wrote him: "The dastardly outrage of which you are the victim is an attack upon the liberty of every citizen of this Republic. It cries to Heaven to rebuke the tyranny that dares attempt to abridge the sacred right of free speech." Privately, James A. Peterson, La Follette's oldest Minnesota friend, wrote that he could not send La Follette a list of antiwar Minnesotans because "The State of Minnesota is practically in a state of siege — patriots have organized every precinct in the State — the sleuths are watching every move that is made here."

La Follette shared the movement's fear of where the government and vigilantes would strike next. He knew the government read his mail, and there were times, like June 20, 1917, when no mail was delivered and he feared none would be again. "These are trying times," he wrote a Wisconsin lieutenant: "Do not write me, except in parables and innuendo." He was extremely careful that *La Follette's* not violate censors' regulations, but feared suppression at any time. In fact, the Post Office did investigate the magazine in August 1918, but did not act.

He grew accustomed to the glares of fellow streetcar passengers and the occasional one that spat on him. He expected the next editorial that would brand him a traitor. But he was cut deeply by the petition signed by 421 faculty members of the University of Wisconsin in January 1918, deploring "his failure loyally to support the government in the prosecution of the war." The faculty was composed of the devoted modernizers of the Wisconsin Idea. Their petition hurt more than the Wisconsin legislature's 1918 condemnation of him for sedition.

The struggle against Wilson's war policies and the fear of government and vigilante repression subtly but profoundly influenced the personalities of La Follette and other antiwar leaders. "One of the hardest things about the last two years," La Follette wrote the family in December 1918, "is the feeling of repression we have to carry around with us. . . . I know it has made me a very different person to live with." Fola wrote simply that "one doesn't feel free to write much of what is in our hearts." This inner sense of repression would have one of two results. La Follette believed that "it is the suppressed emotion of the masses that breeds revolution." The other possibility was that people would liberate their long-repressed feelings by overthrowing all traditional restraints and expressing themselves more fully in private.

In homes away from Washington a great many, perhaps a majority, quietly agreed with La Follette but dared not express their views. Afraid to speak in public, they developed an even more reverential attitude toward leaders who said what they felt. At a meeting of Wisconsin school superintendents, Nicholas Gunderson, Prairie du Chien superintendent, voted against a resolution demanding La Follette's expulsion from the Senate. When the chairman asked him to make the vote unanimous, Gunderson stood up and said, "Robert M. La Follette has championed the cause of the common people for too many years for me . . . to vote for his expulsion. . . . I vote NO!" After the meeting broke up, Mary Bradford, Kenosha superintendent, told Gunderson, "I am proud of you. Many would have liked to have voted with you, but we didn't dare to." The Mary Bradfords of America developed profound admiration for the Nicholas Gundersons and Robert La Follettes.

This theme ran through the mail that descended on La Follette. One-third of all the letters he received during his nineteen years in the Senate came in 1917 in support of his antiwar campaign. A sample ran 67 to 1 in his favor. The growing number of workers whom corporate-oriented modernization had made class-conscious wrote their approval. Local unions in Seattle; Chicago; Shelburn, Indiana; Miami, Arizona; Decatur, Illinois; and San Francisco formally praised his stand. George Anderson of Denver wrote that "a large majority of the working class endorses your stand." The correspondents among workers supported La Follette because he was resisting a capitalist war and trying to shift its burdens to the rich, and because they were the main victims of the campaign against free speech and assembly.

As strong as the class tie was the ethnic bond that made German-Americans reluctant to kill people who might be their relatives. Before the war declaration, German-American groups warmly praised La Follette, but they became much more circumspect after the declaration. Many quietly adopted the charge that it was a capitalist war, because this was the most frequent critical theme, and they found their only support among workers and farmers. In Minnesota, Germans united with militant farmers and workers to overthrow the corporate superpatriots who ran that state.

Many farmers felt particularly isolated and became more and more angry at the middlemen whose profits soared with the war. The president of the Farmers Union reported to La Follette that western and southern farmers opposed the war by a nine-to-one margin. Robert Bell, of Sweet Gum, Georgia, "a goober-grabbler reared up in the back woods," typified the farm supporters who wrote La Follette a word of cheer. R. M. Britt of Wesson, Arkansas, told La Follette that he had the support of the "farmers, to a man."

The war meant the wrenching of husbands, brothers, and sons into frightful, potentially immoral new places. Many had come to America to escape this enforced destruction of families by the state. Many of La Follette's correspondents doubted whether family discipline would outlive the war. "I absolutely will not give him to this unjust war even though they kill us both," wrote Mrs. J. H. Allen of Indianapolis.

But all the writers insisted that La Follette was fighting their fight, that he was the courageous patriot and spokesman of the majority. The leaders had "lost their heads and betrayed the interests of the great mass of the population," wrote Emanuel Amdursky. "Your patriotism must have inspired every unselfish and true American," wrote a Chicago doctor.

Receiving hundreds of similar letters daily, La Follette naturally believed those who told him that the majority supported him. A doctor in Newark, New Jersey, reported that all his patients opposed the war. La Follette also learned that most Massachusetts voters supported his stand and that "The plain people" of Callman, Alabama, "are not for this war." Election returns seemed to support these claims. The Chicago alderman who received the largest plurality in 1917 was the city's most outspoken antiwar alderman, opposed by every newspaper in the city. In the summer of 1917, North Dakota elected a new congressman who demanded conscription of the wealthy. Dayton, Ohio, residents repudiated corporate control of both major parties by voting overwhelmingly for Socialist officials, and the Socialist candidate for mayor of New York fared better than any other radical had in 34 years. La Follette rebuked friends who believed that the majority supported the war hysteria.

The crisis fundamentally altered insurgency at a time when it probably had more popular support than ever before. "The right kind of sentiment is seething and boiling beneath the surface," observed La Follette's son Bob. The people "are talking and thinking but not out loud because of fear of persecution." Convinced of majority support but denied any forum from which to speak, the insurgents decided to direct their energies toward recapturing the rights of free speech, free press, and free assembly. La Follette had only his magazine and the Senate to communicate with a majority that may well have been more sympathetic to him than it had been in 1907. No official body dared invite him to speak. A hostile press now ridiculed and distorted his words. A potential constituency far greater than a decade earlier accepted his views on the war, the draft, the profiteers, the cost of living, and taxes, but La Follette and other insurgents had first to tear down the barrier of suppression that prevented constituents and leaders from uniting on such substantive issues.

The best method, La Follette concluded, was to insist on the right of individuals to express their views. He counterattacked the press because even a campaign for free speech would fail if newspapers continually called him a traitor. He sued the *Madison Democrat* in November 1917 and the *Wisconsin State Journal* in January 1918 for libeling him. Although the suits ultimately dragged on to no conclusion, they revealed the fundamental problem in the decision to emphasize civil liberties. Phil La Follette warned his father that if he won the damage suits he would lose the support of people who admired him precisely because he was like them, a powerless victim of the war machine. The average citizen could not secure redress by filing libel suits.

Although La Follette always viewed the campaign for free speech as a necessary means of allowing the majority to fight its rulers, many other civil libertarians saw the campaign as self-protection from a hostile environment. They were not always certain whether the hostile force was a ruling elite or the majority itself. Insurgency's greatest force, its sense of democratic majoritarianism, was ebbing before its greatest challenge, the inability of the individual to make himself heard. The result would be a new elitist tone in many reformist intellectuals.

La Follette himself was still being investigated by a Senate committee to determine whether he was still entitled to his seat, and as a result remained in the background throughout much of 1918. From the start most committee members wanted an excuse to bury the issue. The committee delayed action until the war ended, and in December 1918 voted 9 to 2 to dismiss the charges. Chairman Atlee Pomerene of Ohio, sharing Wilson's hatred of La Follette, presented a minority report to the Senate in January 1919 which was defeated 50 to 21. Three years later the Senate acknowledged its shame in taking seriously what by then seemed the frivolous charge of treason against La Follette; it reimbursed the senator $5000 for his legal expenses.

Toward the end of the war both the Wilson Administration and the large corporations that had played such a conspicuous part in the war effort became frightened by the outbreak of revolutions in Europe and the symptoms of revolution at home. In 1918 Wilson ordered American troops into Russia, where they joined British and other Allied forces in a de facto war against the Bolsheviks' revolutionary regime; and at Versailles the president joined Allied leaders in seeking a settlement that would contain the spread of revolution. La Follette and the insurgents, by contrast, warmly championed the Bolshevik cause because the Russians, as La Follette wrote, were "struggling to establish an industrial democracy." War-weary soldiers were returning home to join with workers and farmers to overthrow the leaders who had caused the war. Wilson and the other Allied politicians at Versailles were committing "the crime of all crimes against democracy" by sending troops to suppress the Bolsheviks while putting down movements for self-determination in such countries as Ireland and Egypt.

La Follette supported Hiram Johnson's resolution demanding the withdrawal of American troops from Russia, a resolution that failed by one vote in February 1919. Throughout 1919 he charged that Wilson's opposition to Bolshevism was fundamentally grounded not in a hatred for the Bolsheviks' execution of political enemies, as Wilson claimed, but in the fear that a socialist government based on common ownership of property might export its model. Wilson's conception of the right of peoples to choose their governments was bounded, as in Mexico earlier, by the assumptions that the form be capitalist and the crucial ingredient be the promotion of economic growth. Wilson and other Democrats thus embraced the corporations' campaign to suppress Bolshevism in the United States.

La Follette watched the growing official suppression of Bolsheviks and radicals in 1919 and 1920 with a mounting fear that the Red Scare was simply a continuation of the wartime campaign against corporate critics. Attorney General A. Mitchell Palmer arrested and deported hundreds of radicals, suppressed radical meetings, and campaigned for peacetime antisedition laws. Businessmen forced the suspension of a Washington teacher, a friend of La Follette's, for "disloyal utterances" when she said that Bolshevism might be appropriate for the Russian people.

"Just how the public is to protect itself against this thing I am not able to see at present," he confessed in April 1919. He and other insurgents fought hard to repeal the Espionage Act, "the greatest crime of this war," under which political prisoners were charged. His resolution to repeal the act lost by a 39-to-25 vote, with 31 of the 33 voting Democrats siding with their president to preserve this instrument of repression. La Follette also championed better treatment for imprisoned conscientious objectors and a pardon for Socialist leader Eugene V. Debs, whom the government had prosecuted under the Espionage Act in the waning weeks of the war and whom Wilson persisted in viewing as a "traitor" for the rest of his life. He helped defeat the administration's peacetime sedition bill. He promoted full amnesty for all political prisoners. At the same time that he was campaigning for civil liberties, however, he felt that free discussion was a casualty in the struggle between repressive officials and the repressed radicals who had no alternative but violence and bombs. "One fool bomber can sweep aside with a single bomb the effect of months of intelligent work and cards of arguments for free speech."

The campaigns against American policy toward Russia and against domestic repression led La Follette into strong opposition to the League of Nations. Unlike many conservatives who were against any restrictions on American freedom of action, La Follette had long supported the idea of international cooperation. But he believed that the Versailles Treaty was a reactionary document designed to suppress movements for popular democracy that were erupting throughout the world in the war's aftermath. Wilson and the Allies, he charged, wanted to "build an iron ring of conservative governments about her and wall in the dangerous doctrines of the Soviet government." Wilson and the Allies further wanted to protect the dominant financial interests in their countries from revolution. La Follette's vision of a future world order, on the other hand, was one without armaments, without imperialism, without conscription, one in which the people voted before they went to war. "We don't need to restrain the peoples of different countries from making war upon each other. We do need to restrain the ruling classes of every country, from inciting or compelling its people to war upon those of some other country," he explained in the magazine. As the champion of people's rights to choose their own governments even by revolution, La Follette became a focal point for groups protesting the treaty's refusal to give them self-government. Initially supporting recognition for the Soviets, he soon became a champion of independence for Ireland, India, China, and Egypt, receiving material for his speeches from such groups as the American Association for the Recognition of the Irish Republic, the India Home Rule League, and the Chinese Defense League.

He developed his independent position on the Senate floor. He had refused in March to sign a Republican protest against the treaty's terms because the conservatives who prepared the protest had not attacked the treaty's assumptions. He fought first to strike out the labor provisions because "the practical effect . . . is to crystallize the present industrial conditions and to perpetuate the wrong and injustice in the present relation existing between labor and capital." The Senate retained the labor provisions by a 47-to-34 vote.

He arraigned the treaty for violating the principle of self-government by denying the right of revolution and ignoring longstanding differences between peoples it threw together. "The little group of men who sat . . . at Versailles were not peacemakers. They were war makers. They cut and slashed the map of the Old World. . . . They locked the chains on the subject peoples of Ireland, Egypt, and India. . . . Then, fearing the wrath of outraged peoples, . . . they made a league of nations to stand guard over the swag!" La Follette then introduced six reservations to the treaty which accentuated his differences with conservative Republicans. The reservations, all of which were resoundingly defeated but most of which had the support of the remaining insurgent Republicans, granted the right of revolution; demanded that all member states abolish conscription, enact advisory war referenda, cut their arms spending by 80 per cent, and ban any annexation of territory; and prohibited exploitation of the natural resources of weaker counties.

La Follette then voted against the treaty as Republican leaders like Henry Cabot Lodge proposed to amend it and against the treaty as Wilson had submitted it. The final vote put him in the company of insurgent and conservative Republicans alike. Democratic floor leader Hitchcock roasted La Follette because "he voted against war, and now he votes against peace," and the Democratic National Committee called La Follette the general who commanded the "Battalion of Death" that killed the treaty. La Follette believed that the credit belonged to fellow insurgents — Borah, Johnson, and Reed — whose denunciations had stirred the voters.

In fighting Wilson and the treaty, La Follette increasingly defended the rights of Congress as a means of dramatizing his larger battle for free speech. He linked the cause of radicals at home with that of Congress, both victims of "Wilsonian autocracy." La Follette charged publicly in 1919 that Wilson was "the greatest autocrat in the world" who had "outgrown the constitutional limits of the office" by usurping the powers of Congress, a charge made meaningful to infuriated conservative Republicans when Wilson implied on the eve of the 1918 elections that they had been disloyal. He privately believed that the president "just about deserves impeachment."

It was natural for a senator whose civil liberties had been suppressed to believe that the best way to restore free discussion was for Congress to regain its power. But this belief allied him to the majority faction of the majority party in Congress, the conservative Republicans, who would wield the power he was urging Congress to seize. Realizing this, he carefully established his independence. When the new Republican-controlled Senate convened in May 1919, he rejected Penrose's offer of the second highest spot on the powerful committee that determined which bills would reach the Senate floor. "I don't want the responsibility even in a left-handed way for the business this Congress — or the Senate end of it is likely to do," he explained to his family.

During his attack on the treaty La Follette never forgot that a basic part of his fight against the League and for free speech was to persuade the Senate to regain its power from President Wilson. La Follette goaded the Senate to reassert its authority: "We have been trained for two years during the war . . . to jump through the hoop and . . . lie down and roll over whenever the President said so, until the Senate of the United States . . . has become an abject and subservient body." Wilson was trying to "bully" the Senate.

The fight against the treaty climaxed La Follette's campaign to reassert the constitutional rights of the war's victims, whether workers, war critics, or the Senate itself. He had demanded the right to be heard, for himself and for the Senate, and the Senate had asserted that right in killing Wilson's treaty. The most significant result was perhaps subtly to encourage people to throw off their wartime fears. The presidential war machine had forced people to conform and remain silent, to be "cringing" and "abject" like the Senate. It was a declaration of independence that inspired more than senators.

The forces that merged to defeat Wilsonian internationalism reflected a general popular suspicion of rhetorical idealism, a feature of prewar progressivism. "Democracy" was an empty slogan to people who had just made "the world safe for democracy" only to discover that the result was to suppress democracy at home and abroad. Americans wanted no more rhetoric. They were again interested in local and immediate problems — their economic plight, their jobs, their families, their class. They shunned rhetoric about the "unity" of all citizens. Before the war, insurgents had appealed to patriotism and a sense of a united community in seeking to restrain corporate power. During the war, however, the administration and its conservative allies had used similar rhetoric in the service of corporate domination and the suppression of popular revolts. The substance of corporate control, not rhetorical legacies, remained the basic reality of postwar America.

As La Follette again established his independent record, he used that record in a new way. During the peak of insurgency, he had wanted roll call votes to expose his enemies' subservience to the interests, to defeat them, but during the war he was more interested in clarifying his own position, establishing his right to be heard. It was the difference between using the record for majoritarian exposure, with the assumption that people already supported his cause, and the individualistic civil liberties approach, with the assumption that popular opinion was either hostile, lacked the means to express itself, or was so divided by ethnic and class conflicts that a unified majority no longer existed. Insurgency was no longer so much a majoritarian movement uniting people across ethnic and class barriers as a movement trying to protect the rights of individuals and minorities within a corporate world of modernization.

VIII

Insurgency in
a Pressure-Group Society
1919–1924

WORLD WAR I shaped both the emerging American political economy and the future of popular protest. The wartime imperative for speedy economic mobilization and the resulting distribution of economic rewards to pressure groups rapidly accelerated the modernizing tendency of businessmen, farmers, and workers to seek relief by organizing with others who shared their markets and jobs. If workers resented wartime high prices in their roles as consumers, through the War Labor Board government urged them to form unions and find relief from those prices in the form of higher wages. The war and conservative Republican electoral victories after 1918 gave business control over the shape of modernization. But these developments also unleashed a militant class struggle, as angry farmers and workers in America and elsewhere in the wartorn world sought to seize power and punish the rulers who had dragged them into war.

Since insurgents like La Follette were the only politicians to challenge those rulers, farmers and workers turned to them even after their militance ebbed. Realizing that resistance to corporation control had shifted even more rapidly than before the war from a consumer-taxpayer movement for political democracy to a farmer-worker movement for economic democracy, insurgents reinterpreted their old programs to fit their new constituents.

La Follette believed that World War I "openly enthroned Big Business in mastery of Government." Since everything had to be sacrificed to increased production, modernizers urged businessmen to combine in order to plan and organize their industries. The War Industries Board removed antitrust barriers to combination and urged manufacturers to pool their products and fix their prices. La Follette attacked the contracts by which government guaranteed profits to businessmen as "the greatest plan ever devised for looting the treasury." Since it was " 'unpatriotic' to criticize the trusts" in wartime, government and business became indistinguishable partners. Taught the benefits of combination, businessmen fought hard after the war to preserve their monopolistic habits and influence over government. Even the National Association of Manufacturers, which had promoted competition before the war, urged an end to competition after the war experience.

Conservative Republicans in Congress and, after 1921, the White House were eager to help their old corporate friends to preserve and expand their wartime gains. Early in his administration Warren Harding invited J. P. Morgan and other financiers to the White House for their advice, the first such public collaboration since insurgency had begun. Harding announced that he favored "more business in government and less government in business." Many wartime bodies of industrialists found that they could continue their monopolistic practices with governmental blessing from the Commerce Department under Harding, Coolidge, and Hoover.

To win popular support, conservative Republicans dusted off the old legend of the self-made man, proclaiming that no governmental restraints should prevent a businessman or his corporation from advancing because, as Calvin Coolidge explained, "wealth is the chief end of man." The appeal worked because Americans were eager to escape their wartime feelings of suppression and restraint. Furthermore, corporate leaders had learned new tactics during the war. They emphasized their role in fulfilling the modernizers' concept of service to the country. Instead of showing a defiant attitude toward consumers and workers as they had before the war, these leaders now relied on public relations to please consumers and on paternalistic personnel managers to please workers.

Before the war La Follette had waged offensive campaigns to limit the existing powers of concentrated corporate wealth, but after the war he was conducting defensive crusades to limit at least some of the new gains that corporations were making and to prevent them from dismantling prewar progressive achievements. Westerners had long fumed at what the *Seattle Times* called "the repressive policies that were adopted by the government at the height of the conservation excitement," and they persuaded their congressmen to join the corporations in encouraging exploitation of mineral resources and water power sites on public lands. Western congressmen therefore promoted two bills in 1919 that created long-term leases for exploitation of coal, oil, and water power.

The leasing bills repealed the heart of the conservation program, La Follette charged, and they stimulated monopoly development because control of natural resources encouraged industrial trusts. Aided by conservation lobbyists Gifford Pinchot and Harry Slattery, La Follette killed the leasing bills with a filibuster before Congress adjourned in 1919. Still thinking of consumers, La Follette protested that the bills would "dispose of all the resources that will furnish heat and energy to the people of the United States for all time to come."

In 1920, however, he failed to prevent the enactment of the Mineral Leasing and Water Power acts, which established fifty-year leases to exploit minerals and water power on public lands. When the Senate overwhelmingly trounced his amendment regulating the prices of minerals and passed the bills, private corporate development expanded tremendously. In the twenty years before the Water Power Act, the government had received applications for sites projecting only 2.5 million horsepower, but in the eight months after the act went into effect, applications totalled 13 million horsepower. The rush for oil leases in 1920 reminded observers of the Oklahoma land rush of 1887, when the government had last thrown a significant part of its land open to private development.

Although La Follette was deeply troubled as he watched Congress repeal prewar achievements in the area of natural resources, he was even more concerned with policy toward railroads. He had long believed that the government's railroad policy offered the best place to experiment with programs that could later be applied to all corporations. On the eve of American entry into World War I he had concluded that regulation by the Interstate Commerce Commission had failed to protect consumers and that government management of the railroads during the war — necessitated by the failure of private management to mobilize men and supplies rapidly enough for the war — was a long step toward permanent government ownership. Although in the immediate postwar period he personally preferred public ownership, he supported the railroad brotherhoods' Plumb Plan because it was the only politically realistic alternative to the owners' plan to restore the railroads to their private owners. The Plumb Plan would have shared management among owners, workers, and the public and would have slashed rates; the resulting lower prices for goods shipped on trains would allow workers to buy more goods and thus create more jobs.

La Follette, therefore, bitterly resisted the Esch-Cummins Transportation Act of 1920. It was little more than a 1916 plan devised by the owners of railroad stocks and bonds. The act returned the railroads to their private owners and guaranteed the railroads a 5 1/2 to 6 per cent return on their securities, which were, in turn, controlled by the Money Trust, at a time when government bonds returned only 4 per cent. Since the face value of the watered securities, not the companies' physical assets, determined the return, La Follette claimed this amounted to a 9 or 10 per cent return on actual property. He further protested the $530 million Federal subsidy to the owners to compensate them for alleged damage suffered during the period of government operation.

La Follette was furious that the act gave the railroads their major objectives since the 1890s, objectives that the progressives had blocked before the war: legalized pooling and guaranteed minimum prices, exempting them from the antitrust laws. He complained that the act severely undercut more radical state regulatory commissions by giving traditional state powers to the more conservative Interstate Commerce Commission. He protested a provision that he feared would prohibit strikes by railroad workers. Finally, he attacked the promised 25 per cent increase in freight rates that would cost the ultimate consumers $4 1/3 billion.

During his long campaign against the Esch-Cummins Act, La Follette realized that he lacked even the vague, unorganized support of consumers and taxpayers that had buoyed his regulation fights from 1905 to 1914, and for the first time in a regulation campaign, he worked closely instead with organized groups of workers and farmers. The railroad brotherhoods pledged "to do anything in their power" to assist him. They broke an old union rule and gave him the names of their members for him to solicit as subscribers to *La Follette's*. The Farmers' National Council, claiming to represent 750,000 farmers, and the leaders of the Farmers' Union, the Grange, and the Equity Society issued a bulletin condemning the act.

The railroads' signal victory in 1920 was especially galling to La Follette since former insurgent Albert Cummins of Iowa, swept along by his party's growing conservatism, had helped to engineer it. Old-time insurgency had clearly dissolved.

Although La Follette failed to modify the act's provisions, he did make it a major issue in political campaigns of the early 1920s. He exposed the railroads' $3 million public relations campaign to discredit government operation of the railroads. As he spearheaded the movement among labor and farm groups to defeat legislators who had supported the act, La Follette received ammunition for his charges of collusion between government and business in August 1920 when the ICC granted railroads increases of 35 per cent on freight and 20 per cent on passenger rates. The result was that many congressional supporters of the act, including coauthor John J. Esch of Wisconsin, were defeated in November.

The railroad and leasing laws of 1920 repealed significant prewar progressive achievements. They reflected a corporation-oriented desire among legislators to encourage production and release restraints. But the 1920 laws also showed La Follette that his future constituents would be job-oriented farmers and workers. When he charged that consumers and taxpayers suffered from the repeal of earlier railroad and conservation policies, no one listened. Mineral and waterpower development meant jobs; thus he found little support for his conservation campaign. But farmers agreed with his railroad fight because higher freight rates hurt them as shippers, and workers supported him because they wanted a larger voice in railroad management.

The replacement of prewar consumer and taxpayer support for La Follette's regulation fight by worker and farmer backing was part of a larger process. Consumer and taxpayer consciousness was disappearing before a mighty uprising of angry farmers and workers whose class consciousness had grown quietly during wartime's official suppression. The war had encouraged Americans to think as producers, not consumers, and to find relief for their problems in job-oriented groups. If workers felt angry about food prices, they should form unions that rewarded them with higher wages so long as they kept producing. Farmers should feel glad for guaranteed prices at unfamiliarly high levels.

La Follette was not surprised when both groups fought militantly to preserve their wartime gains in the face of inflation, collapsing farm prices, depression, and corporate refusals to grant pay raises. They demanded greater control over the productive process, a larger return for their labors in field and factory. "The movement for democracy in industry," La Follette explained in 1919, "is tending to supersede at many points the old struggle for political democracy." Until this new outbreak of job-oriented militance, La Follette had retained hope for rekindling consumer-taxpayer support for insurgency. This postwar movement dramatized the extent to which Americans had apparently switched their loyalties to their jobs.

Workers expressed their new militance so vehemently in 1919 that conservatives feared the revolution had arrived. Nearly 21 per cent of all American workers struck their employers in 1919, five times more than in an average prewar year. They created organizations to discipline their employers and, if necessary, older, more conservative union leaders. John L. Lewis tried to dampen the grassroots militance of coal miners in 1919 by expelling 81 locals in Kansas and 24 in Illinois from the United Mine Workers. Chicago railroad workers seized upon a minor incident early in 1920 as an excuse for a wildcat strike, and the brotherhood leaders, fearing rebellion from below, recruited strikebreakers to replace the striking workers. Union officers resisted grassroots campaigns by women teachers and printers. Steelworkers, without a union since 1892, rebelled against their employers and struck from September 1919 until early 1920. Policemen in Boston walked off their jobs when their demands for unionization were not met.

While many workers risked their lives in bitter struggles with employers, many others advocated working-class political action. Beginning at Bridgeport, Connecticut, in September 1918, rank-and-file workers formed local labor parties. Despite bitter opposition from Samuel Gompers and the AFL, workers

— particularly coal miners — forced state federations of labor in Pennsylvania and Indiana to endorse the principle of a class party in 1919. The national Labor Party was organized in 1919 and declared that "throughout the world workers have reached the determination to . . . take control of their own lives and their government."

The militance of labor was paralleled by growing discontent among farmers. The collapse of farm markets, the end of wartime regulations over the food industry and of guaranteed farm prices, and the Federal Reserve Board's deflationary policy had produced a depression in agriculture, which isolated farmers from the urban prosperity of the 1920s. Gross farm income shrank from $17.7 billion in 1919 to $10.5 billion in 1921. Because they were trying to preserve family discipline and evangelical religion during a decade of unparalleled generational conflict and secularization, the farmers' sense of isolation and their militancy were increased.

Desperate farmers sought new ways to receive a larger share of the ultimate selling price of their products. Gronna complained in 1920 that wheat farmers received only one-fourth of the price consumers paid for bread. By 1921 Senator E. F. Ladd of North Dakota proclaimed through *La Follette's* that "the farmer in the past, largely individualistic in his habits, business, and thinking, at last finds himself no longer able as an individual to cope with organized business." Realizing that, as a class, they were the largest single group of producers, they were uniting to control their market.

The revolts by farmers and workers found common ground soon after the war ended. Both felt that middlemen prevented them from receiving a larger share of the product of their labor. Early in 1919 La Follette learned that farmers and workers were forming a common movement in the state of Washington. A new Farmer-Labor Cooperative Association formed at Kenosha, Wisconsin, "to try to eliminate the middlemen and reduce the high cost of living." The president of the Appleton Trades and Labor Council joined with the county's Nonpartisan League, together representing "the organized laborers and farmers" of the Fox River Valley, to ask La Follette to address them in 1920. By 1920 La Follette believed that farmers and workers had united so rapidly in the months since the war's end that "there are only two classes, 'the autocratic plutocrats,' and 'the farmers and workers,'" and that future political radicalism would have to be job-oriented.

The presidential campaign of 1920 would test the farmer-worker revolt. La Follette, eager to lead farmers and workers to victory, wrote a platform that would rally all opponents of corporate modernization. The platform evoked memories of wartime suppression, pledging repeal of the Espionage and Sedition acts, restoration of civil liberties, and abolition of the draft. It promised ultimate government ownership of the rail-roads, natural resources, and agricultural processing opera-tions. It urged government sponsorship of farmer and worker organizations to achieve "collective bargaining" to control the products of their work.

La Follette tested the platform's appeal at the April Wis-consin election that chose delegates to the Republican presi-dential convention. Although his delegates carried the state by a 50,000-vote margin, the Wisconsin delegation soon dis-covered that it was alone in the Republican convention. Con-servative Senate leaders bossed it completely, and Oswald Garrison Villard wondered "how business could be going on in Wall Street when so many of its most distinguished figures were in Chicago" for the convention. When Edward J. Gross read La Follette's plank demanding repeal of the Esch-Cummins Act, he was drowned out by boos, hisses, and cries of "Bolshevik!" The Wisconsin delegates retaliated by jumping on their chairs and bellowing their opposition when the con-vention sought unanimous support for Harding's nomination.

Rejected by the Republicans, La Follette worked with leaders trying to create a third party that, unlike Republicans and Democrats, would be free from corporation control. The fledgling Labor Party held a convention at Chicago in mid-July at the same time as a convention made up of middle-class inheritors of Roosevelt's Progressive Party. Both groups wanted La Follette to lead a third-party presidential campaign, and he consented if they could agree on a platform similar to Wisconsin's at the GOP convention.

Both conventions appointed subcommittees to write a joint platform, but the committees fought all night without agreeing on the plank pledging industrial democracy. Behind their fight were the class jealousies that racked postwar radical movements. The prewar commitment to political democracy, when challenged by the class struggle of 1918–1920, turned out to mean economic democracy to farm and labor leaders and civil liberties to the old middle-class progressives. The Labor leaders at Chicago blamed the failure to agree on the progressives' obsession with respectability, and the progressives blamed it on the class prejudices of Labor spokesmen.

Many delegates to both conventions were disgusted with their leaders for failing to see that there was a common enemy, corporate control of government, and a common friend, Bob La Follette. When leaders told the progressive convention of their failure to produce an acceptable platform, the majority of delegates stomped out to join the Labor convention. When the Labor chairman announced the same news, a delegate stood up, declared that La Follette's platform was fine, and amid great cheering a red banner lettered in white with "Bob La Follette" unfurled over the balcony. Delegates would have overruled their leaders had not Robert, Jr. announced at that point that his father could not run without platform agreement. Because La Follette was both respectable and an outcast at the same time, because he was more often identified as a fighter than he was with postwar ideologies, he was popular with both groups. Whatever had happened at Chicago, many components of the farmer-worker alliance, including the Farmer-Labor Party in Minnesota and the Triple

Alliance of unions, railway brotherhoods, and farmers in Washington, expected him to lead in the future.

The class tensions that aborted La Follette's presidential campaign showed that the insurgents' prewar faith in uniting people by a common faith in political democracy was meaningless to job-oriented postwar America. Other common values that had permitted people to unite across social barriers were equally threatened after the war. Prewar Americans had agreed that family obligations were the root of social unity, but the war, by suddenly uprooting husbands and sons and exposing them to horrible violence, vastly accelerated the erosion of Victorian family discipline that had begun with industrialism.

La Follette had experienced this generational battle earlier. In 1911 his daughter Fola, a second-line actress, announced that she was going to marry an easygoing playwright, George Middleton. Belle was shocked; Middleton differed completely from Robert La Follette. But Fola disliked her parents' Victorian attitudes of self-denial and sensory deprivation. They did not relax or express their feelings freely enough. "They never let up and play for a few glad hours," Fola complained to her brother Robert. They did not feel the joy of making love. In the end Fola did marry Middleton, and her parents accepted him by giving him a column in La Follette's that made him part of the cause.

Ten years later, as people expressed feelings suppressed by the war, the revolt first expressed by Fola and her self-conscious Bohemian friends in New York swept the country. Isabelle Bacon recalled that she and Phil La Follette had spent hours during their 1920–1921 courtship "discoursing on how to retain the greatest amount of freedom." Her parents "could not understand" the new " 'freedom' in the atmosphere." Phil's worry over what his marriage to Isabelle would do to his freedom, would have been unthinkable for his parents. Family discipline, an unwritten assumption that had encouraged people before the war to find other bases of unity in insurgency, did not survive.

Other social areas reverberated after the war to unparalleled sounds of battle. In December 1918 suffragists burned Wilson's words promising self-determination in a procession joined by thousands. La Follette started the applause on the Senate floor in June 1919 when the Senate enacted woman suffrage, and he attacked the "damned social customs" that deprived women of equal rights with men. Blacks who risked death for democracy abroad and experienced newfound equality in France were furious when they returned home to find whites fighting to preserve prewar jobs and the system of segregation. In the summer of 1919, racial tensions erupted into 26 riots, and La Follette was appalled that white soldiers spearheaded many of them. As women and blacks demanded rights implied by a war for democracy, they stimulated men and whites to fight to preserve older values.

Finally, the war and its aftermath created new meanings for consumers and community loyalty, underpinnings of prewar insurgency. The war, La Follette realized, bred "distrust and suspicion among neighbors" of different backgrounds. The sudden imposition of the loyalty yardstick compelled people to behave outwardly in ways they had not believed inwardly. Since trust between neighbors had evaporated, the ideal of the united community of consumers lost its meaning. Divisions between young and old, worker and employer, black and white, man and woman, farmer and city-dweller were more important than unity as consumers and taxpayers.

The fragmentation of consumers into bitterly warring camps also challenged modernizers, for manufacturers were producing goods at an unprecedented rate in the 1920s by widely adopting the movable assembly line. They needed consumers who had a common enough meeting ground that they would buy the same products. The solution came through the rapid development of new mass media — radio and movies —

and new heroes — sports stars and entertainers — who could provide new common denominators for consumers. In the resulting world, where community loyalty degenerated into Babbittry, the town muckraker, as in *Babbitt,* quickly took a job from the people he had been exposing and attacked their critics. Consumers were too divided by their other loyalties to resist, and the latest movie star or sports hero united them as insurgents had before the war. It was a unity that, unlike insurgency, required no greater risk or commitment than to comment on Babe Ruth or Charlie Chaplin. Such comments were the only safe ones in the socially divisive climate that the war had created.

La Follette, less interested in these social changes than in disciplining corporate power, saw that farmers and workers were his best hope. But he also saw that farmers and workers, while remaining job-oriented, were losing much of the angry militance of 1919 and 1920 and turning more toward particular pressure groups. As he had learned in his presidential campaign, the new radical leaders often disillusioned their followers by their bitter quarrels. Precisely their faith that workers would soon dethrone capitalists had caused ferocious leadership struggles over the desirability of revolutionary unionism, political strikes, and Bolshevism. While leaders battled over the best direction for the new class consciousness, workers in particular industries faced problems that dictated pressure-group action instead of class action. The prospect of prohibition drove brewery workers, with a long radical tradition, into an alliance with their employers. The debate over railroad policy intensified group consciousness among railroad workers. Finally, the failure of most strikes in 1919, like that among steelworkers led by the radical William Z. Foster, soured many workers on militant action.

When a depression hit in 1921, farmers and workers sought immediate relief from Congress through old and new pressure groups. The sudden growth of the American Farm Bureau

Federation, from its birth in 1919 to one million members by 1920, and the formal creation of a farm bloc among congressmen in May 1921 showed farmers' newfound determination to influence policy. Numbering 20 to 25 senators and nearly 100 congressmen, the farm bloc, including La Follette, piled up an impressive record in relieving its constituents from the agricultural depression, including tariff relief, Federal farm loans, nominal regulation of middlemen, and price-fixing by agricultural cooperatives.

More radical farmer and worker groups created a common lobbying ground in the People's Legislative Service, and La Follette became its most prominent leader. La Follette was always interested in sufficient financing before he led a movement, and the PLS received its funds from the railroad brotherhoods and William T. Rawleigh, a wealthy patent medicine manufacturer from Illinois who had grown up in Wisconsin and worshipped La Follette. He became the senator's financial angel after 1919, financing political campaigns, visits to a sanitarium, and a trip to Europe.

The PLS began in the election of 1920 when the brotherhoods worked with the AFL, the Nonpartisan League, and other farm groups to elect congressmen who would repeal the Esch-Cummins Act. La Follette and PLS director Basil Manly prepared with union and farm spokesmen for a congressional dinner on April 17, 1921, when the PLS was formally launched. La Follette gave the keynote address, emphasizing his old insurgent theme that wealth influenced politics, a theme echoed by the other speakers, Vice-Chairman Democratic Congressman George Huddleston of Alabama, George W. Norris, and Democratic Senator David Walsh of Massachusetts.

Many prewar insurgents, believing that farmer-labor cooperation was now the only way to dethrone corporate control of government, joined the PLS, including Jane Addams, Fred Howe, Florence Kelley, and Edward A. Ross. Beginning in February 1922, *La Follette's* carried Manly's column, "On Guard for the People," exposing corporate influence over particular bills. In contrast to the Farm Bureau, whose emphasis was on lobbying, the PLS researched issues for individual legislators and distributed their speeches. The PLS assisted La Follette's 1921 and 1922 Senate attacks on the wage, rate, and securities practices of the railroads, the attempts by the Justice Department to emasculate the Federal Trade Commission, and the open-shop and antistrike campaigns of prominent business groups.

La Follette continued to believe that taxation was the best way to redistribute wealth. Although he had attacked the 1917 and 1918 revenue acts because they did not tax excess profits or surplus incomes enough, he was forced to defend those acts in 1921 when Treasury Secretary Andrew Mellon demanded their repeal because they restrained corporate initiative and business prosperity. He worked closely with his bitterest tax enemy of 1917, Furnifold Simmons of North Carolina, to resist Mellon's plan. La Follette sought an amendment requiring publicity of tax returns to expose wealthy tax-dodgers, but conservative Republicans defeated it. They also succeeded in removing some of the steepest wartime taxes on incomes and profits. La Follette and Simmons, however, defeated a provision that would have exempted individuals and corporations who made their money in overseas operations, saving taxpayers about a quarter of a billion dollars. Farmer and worker legislators were powerful enough in 1921 to win a gift tax. When Coolidge assisted Mellon's tax program in 1924, La Follette and his allies failed to prevent still further cuts in taxes on high incomes, but did succeed in levying a stiff gift tax, raising the estate tax from 25 to 40 per cent, and requiring full publicity of tax returns.

La Follette's cooperation with Simmons and other Democrats in 1921 and 1924 underscored the conservative Republicans' complete control of modernization. It also showed that taxes, a prominent basis for unity among classes in prewar insurgency, had become even more a class and interest-group issue than during the war. Organized farmers and workers resisted the tax burden conservatives were trying to place on their shoulders in the 1920s. Simmons and the Democratic modernizers never shared the enthusiasm of La Follette and the insurgents for taxation as a weapon to redistribute wealth, but they did believe that all groups should contribute to the costs of government and that Mellon was destroying the balance between groups. Arguing that Mellon's program would transfer the tax burden "to those whose industry and productivity are essential to the nation's prosperity," La Follette appealed to farmers' and workers' job-oriented fears of depression as the only hope for widespread support.

La Follette reinterpreted insurgency even more dramatically to support modernizing farmer and worker groups during the tariff debate of 1922. Before that debate, he had consistently argued that lower duties helped consumers over producers and competition over monopoly and provided tax relief for the majority. In 1922, however, instead of reading briefs for the housewife, La Follette emphasized the tariff's effect on workers. He assumed that the most realistic way for workers to fight inflation was by higher wages, not lower prices. "Labor never gets any benefit from a tariff if the manufacturers can prevent it," he charged, and he attacked the Republicans' basic protectionist claim that high duties protected the American worker. He showed that manufacturers did not pass on to workers the extra profits they made from tariff-protected high prices. La Follette voted against the Fordney-McCumber Tariff of 1922 to help Americans in their jobs, a stark reminder of the collapse of consumer consciousness. La Follette was joined by only two other prewar insurgent Republicans in voting against the 1922 tariff, an equally dramatic sign of the collapse of insurgency as an organized movement, since it had been the Payne-Aldrich Tariff of 1909 that had given insurgents their greatest sense of a common movement.

Economic recession provided the setting for the elections of 1922. The PLS organized a convention at Chicago in February 1922, inviting labor and farm leaders, Socialists, the Nonpartisan League, and others "to establish closer understanding" in electing legislators who would resist conservative Republicans. Calling themselves the Conference for Progressive Political Action, the movement that began at Chicago formed branches in 32 states to elect "progressive" candidates.

La Follette was, of course, most interested in his own reelection. Harding denied him patronage, and the Republican National Committee tried to defeat his renomination. La Follette frankly appealed to farmers and workers, "the productive elements of the community," who now suffered a depression because of conservative Republican policies. He easily won renomination with 72 per cent of the vote and reelection with 83 per cent. As ever, he ran best in traditional Republican rural and Scandinavian areas, but, as in 1916, his greatest gains were among Germans and city-dwellers.

La Follette pictured his reelection as part of his leadership of a national farmer-worker movement that would overthrow conservative Republicans, as insurgency had in 1910. He spoke in North Dakota for the Nonpartisan League's senatorial candidate, Lynn Frazier, who faced combined opposition from Democratic and Republican conservatives. But the most dramatic moment of 1922 came when he stumped Minnesota to support Farmer-Labor senatorial candidate Henrik Shipstead against the conservative Republican incumbent, Frank Kellogg, the man who had introduced the resolution to expel La Follette from the Senate in 1917. Conservative newspapers warned Minnesotans against the traitor's return to the same St. Paul auditorium where five years earlier he had so profoundly shaken conservatives. As he and his son Phil approached the auditorium that icy November night in 1922, they found the streets jammed with 25,000 people who could not fit inside. After roasting corporate control over politics, announcing that he did not regret a word he had spoken five years earlier, reading Kellogg's conservative roll call votes, and endorsing Shipstead, he sensed that the audience wanted a further attack on Kellogg, a man who walked with a stoop. He gave them the most vicious characterization in his career: "God Almighty through nature writes men's characters on their faces and in their forms. Your Senator has bowed obsequiously to wealth and to corporations' orders and to his masters until God Almighty has given him a hump on his back — crouching, cringing, un-American, unmanly." When he and Phil returned to the hotel, La Follette mused, "Your mother will give me hell for saying that about Kellogg." She did. But Shipstead won.

By the time the votes were counted in 1922, the *New York Times* observed that La Follette, "leader of the radical-progressives, [would] be the most powerful legislative factor in the next Congress." The organization of farmers and workers had succeeded! The Republican majority in the House shrank from 169 to less than 20, and in the Senate from 24 to 10. As in 1910, legislative progressives, as they now called themselves, held the balance of power. When La Follette convened the new PLS group to plan strategy in December of 1922, 17 senators and 38 congressmen indicated support. In mid-1923 La Follette intervened in a special senatorial election in Minnesota billed by the press as a test between him and Harding, and his candidate, Farmer-Laborite Magnus Johnson, won.

Although La Follette compared the stunning triumphs of 1922–1923 with the insurgent success in 1910, the new victories actually confirmed his emergence as a spokesman for labor and agricultural interest groups. The Senator himself increasingly identified majority rule with such organizations. Thus he attacked the ship subsidy bill of 1922 by arguing that it was opposed by the Farmers Union, Equity, Grange, National Board of Farm Organizations, Farmers National Council, several national unions and state labor federations, and the AFL. The new majority resulted from united action by such pressure groups, since they represented the occupations that provided the livelihood for three-quarters of American families.

La Follette and the new "progressive" group made reform of the Supreme Court one of their first goals. Harding's four conservative appointees to the Court, including the insurgents' old enemy William Howard Taft as Chief Justice, led the Court to strike down many laws that farmers and workers had fought hard to win. The Court twice nullified acts prohibiting child labor, as well as laws prohibiting injunctions in labor disputes, granting minimum wages for working women, and permitting antitrust immunity for labor unions and farm organizations.

When the Court threw out the second child labor act in 1922, La Follette launched his major campaign at the American Federation of Labor convention. "We cannot live under a system of government where we are forced to amend the Constitution every time we want to pass a progressive law," he told the workers' delegates. The Court had nullified a law that had passed both the House and the Senate by better than 80 per cent majorities. La Follette therefore appealed to the AFL to promote a constitutional amendment permitting Congress to override the Court by repassing any law that Court declared unconstitutional. La Follette's proposal, together with the enormous enthusiasm with which union delegates greeted it at the AFL convention, frightened conservatives like Columbia University President Nicholas Murray Butler, who called La Follette an anti-American "revolutionary" because of the proposal.

La Follette's proposal to make Congress superior to the Supreme Court underscored a gradual evolution in his thinking since the war. He was coming to equate the will of the majority with the will of Congress, an evolution that began when he saw the Senate's challenge to Wilson's Versailles Treaty as part of the popular campaign for civil liberties. The majority now spoke through Congress, not direct democracy. And in the 1920s Congress, in turn, was more receptive than the other branches of government to the new interest groups that represented the majority of voters in their job-oriented capacities. During their prewar heyday as confirmed majoritarians, insurgents had proposed a direct popular vote on judicial decisions as the remedy for the courts' conservatism;

in the 1920s they wanted Congress to play the role they had assigned the majority earlier.

La Follette seized upon a major conservative proposal as the opportunity to mold the progressives into "an aggressive group, united upon a program of positive action." On December 9, 1922, the Senate received this scheme after conservative Republicans had steered it through the House. The bill proposed to sell ships that the government had built during the war to private companies for a fraction of their cost and to grant the companies an annual $52 million subsidy. The shipping companies, U.S. Chamber of Commerce, and corporate farmers supported the plan, arguing that the profit motive produced more efficient results than public ownership. La Follette and his fellow progressives conducted a loose filibuster that killed the ship subsidy before adjournment early in 1923, and the new Congress never even considered it. La Follette also rallied progressives in the new Congress to strip Albert Cummins of the chairmanship of the Interstate Commerce Committee as punishment for Cummins' promotion of the hated Esch-Cummins Act, rallying point of the farmer-worker movement.

La Follette and the progressives elected in 1922 fought hard to protect the last effective prewar regulatory agency, the Federal Trade Commission, from conservative raids. La Follette explained that "the farmers, wage-earners and the consuming millions of this country have relied almost entirely in the last decade upon the Federal Trade Commission for protection from ruthless and illegal trusts and monopolies." By threatening an investigation of Attorney General Harry Daugherty in 1922, La Follette had preserved an FTC prohibition on the five major meat-packing companies to keep them from monopolizing the entire food industry. The Senate progressives fought desperately and unsuccessfully in 1925 to block Coolidge's appointment of a corporation lawyer and reactionary to the FTC. "Packed with its [own] worst enemies," as La Follette observed, the FTC overhauled its machinery to benefit corporations charged with unfair trade practices, not their accusers. Corporations now controlled all the prewar regulatory agencies. The collapse of independent regulation cast the progressives adrift from reliance on governmental machinery to redress grievances, and it strengthened their faith that the formation of private, job-oriented interest groups, not government commissions, would redistribute power.

Although La Follette and the new progressives failed in their battle over regulatory agencies, they succeeded in forcing investigations into the growing rumors of corruption in the Harding administration. La Follette had long believed in government ownership of natural resources, and he had earlier preserved the naval oil reserves from private exploitation. On April 28, 1922, La Follette reported tentatively to the Senate that Interior Secretary Albert B. Fall and Navy Secretary Edwin Denby had conspired to lease the oil reserves to private companies, and he declared that he would perfect a resolution demanding an investigation. As he described how Fall had acquired the reserves from Denby and secretly leased the Teapot Dome reserve with its half-billion dollars' worth of oil, senators became interested. Democratic leader Gilbert Hitchcock demanded a quorum call so that other senators could hear La Follette's "shocking surprise" and "amazing revelations." Unwilling to wait for La Follette to perfect his resolution, the Senate passed it on the spot, sensing major discoveries that would include criminal activity by cabinet members sanctioned by the President. But the Teapot Dome investigation floundered until the new legislators elected in 1922 took office. La Follette continued to collect evidence, and the investigation finally took shape when he persuaded Thomas Walsh of Montana to run it in the fall of 1923. By 1923 congressional committees were also investigating the systematic looting of the Veterans' Bureau and the influence-peddling of Attorney General Daugherty.

The 68th Congress, elected in the farmer-worker revolt of

1922, "did more to expose corruption and call public attention to the evils of government in the interests of private monopoly than any of its predecessors," wrote La Follette in 1925. They forced three cabinet members and the head of the Veterans' Bureau from office. In 1924 conservative Republicans counterattacked. Mellon charged that "government business cannot continue to be conducted under frequent interference by investigations of Congress, entirely destructive in their nature." Coolidge and the Republicans responded to investigations by Montana's Burton Wheeler into Attorney General Daugherty's activities and by Michigan's James Couzens into collusion between the Treasury Department and wealthy tax-dodgers by indicting Wheeler for a minor offense in Montana and charging Couzens with underpayment of income taxes.

The Senate was performing the investigative role that the press had played during the era of the muckrakers. The investigations originated from interest groups like the railroad brotherhoods, the PLS, and naval officers, who wanted to use exposure not so much to lead the unorganized majority to challenge the very legitimacy of the malefactor, but to get more for themselves. Most of the mass media, instead of aiding the investigators and developing further and deeper exposures on their own, as they had before the war, now defended the malefactors and the conservative counterattack. The *New York Tribune* called Walsh and Wheeler "the Montana scandalmongers." La Follette might insist that the investigations showed that private monopolies had unprecedented control over government, but the journalists rebuked the charge. Business prosperity caused the economic growth that had pulled the country out of the depression of the early 1920s. In a modernizing world only a scandalmonger would object to prosperity.

La Follette, as a shrewd politician, had discovered that the votes for any real attack on the conservatives would come from organized farmers and workers. But he was still an insurgent, and though he supported interest groups whose concerns were narrowly conceived, he still wanted to dismantle concentrated power and redistribute wealth. Realizing that his new allies believed that economic growth would solve many of their problems, he tried unsuccessfully to persuade them that prosperity itself was impossible on a permanent basis until monopoly and profit prevailed no longer. Uncertain of the best answer, La Follette argued at different times that producer and consumer cooperatives, public ownership, and trust-busting were solutions to the problem of concentrated, private economic power.

La Follette differed fundamentally from conservatives and modernizing interest groups alike, however, in his attitude toward profit. During the 1922 tariff debate he clashed bitterly with George Moses of New Hampshire over the meaning of profit. He and Moses agreed that the huge Amoskeag textile mill in Manchester, New Hampshire, had grown rapidly, opening up new factories that gave new jobs to workers. Moses called the Amoskeag story "the development of a great industrial concern," producing more goods, employing more workers. La Follette then fired the insurgent question that troubled all modernizers, whether progressive or conservative: How had the company acquired the capital to open new mills? La Follette answered that the company "took it out of the public" in the form of excessive prices and profits that became the surplus capital (a fraudulent term to La Follette since the company underpaid its workers), which it invested in new plants. The Amoskeag story was to La Follette "the story of excessive profits that greedy manufacturers can make" when aided by special political privileges like "excessive tariff rates." The additional jobs created by expansion were irrelevant since the new workers would be exploited in their roles as consumers by the very corporation that employed them.

In the twenties La Follette continued to attack the profits acquired by special privileges granted by government to powerful corporations, but he seemed unable to focus clearly on a solution because the new pressure groups did not share his view that concentrated power was the basic evil to attack. At the same time, however, his failure to mount a concerted campaign for any one of his proposals indicated his shrewd realization that his only hope for public support lay in adapting his insurgency to the views of the progressive modernizers.

Presidential Politics and the Death of Insurgency
1924–1925

In the twenties the signs of age began to show on La Follette. His trademarks, the square jaw that had given him his determined look, the pompadour mane of dark hair trailing back from his forehead that had created his fighting appearance of constant movement, and the piercing bright eyes that had made him seem so alert, began to change after the war. The hair became white, the jaw began to sag, and his eyes looked tired, squinting more often. By 1922 the 67-year-old La Follette was known in Wisconsin simply as the "Old Man." In 1924 a reporter observed that his speeches had "mellowed," had lost their "angry power." As his health and age increasingly concerned him, he became friendly for the first time in two decades with people whose ideologies clashed with his own, including such reactionaries as Senator Boies Penrose of Pennsylvania and Senator Henry Cabot Lodge of Massachusetts.

Although he remained devoted to his work, he lost much of the compulsive attitude that had once obsessed him. The PLS researched his speeches, and he no longer felt that each had to be perfect. Although Belle claimed that his magazine was his "recreation," La Follette and his wife now went to the movies often. The senator also became a devotee of murder mysteries, which he devoured with great gusto and speed.

Even in his last years there remained really two La Follettes: a public one, the moralistic zealot, and a private one who listened well to others' feelings and ideas. In 1919 University of Wisconsin philosophy professor Max Otto dreaded his first meeting with La Follette. Otto had watched La Follette's fiery public performances, had heard him mercilessly roast his opponents, and was afraid of the crusading zealot he was about to meet. La Follette entered the room, and Otto recalled: "We shook hands and he looked at me with friendly, affectionate eyes, not at all the platform eyes with which I was familiar. . . . He won me over immediately." His ability to sense other people's feelings and concerns impressed Otto; once La Follette had sensed them, he expressed these concerns in a fearless, slashing oratorical style that impressed audiences and politicians as a unique kind of courageous zeal.

In 1922 he returned to Madison for his first speech there in four years. Friends warned him to ignore the war issue and not revive the old charges that he had been a traitor. La Follette thanked them and began his speech by praising the city where he still lived. Suddenly he raised a clenched fist, shook it, and shouted: "I do not want the vote of a single citizen under any misapprehension of where I stand. I would not change my record on the war for that of any man, living or dead." At first stunned, the audience suddenly erupted into the greatest ovation of La Follette's life. A longtime political enemy shook his head, tears streaming down his cheeks: "I hate the son of a bitch; but, my God, what guts he's got." But it was more than guts that prompted La Follette; he knew what other politicians did not, that the war had been unpopular.

La Follette remained the politician, and he still yearned to be president. Organized farmers and workers might have made major gains in 1922, but those gains did not challenge the essential conservatism of both major parties in the 1920s.

Harding and his cabinet might have given Washington a conservative and corrupt direction, and Coolidge, though honest, might have been even more conservative than Harding, but there was no reason to hope that a Democratic victory would produce any fundamental shifts. After the congressional victories of 1922, the farmer-worker leaders looked to La Follette as the person best capable of reversing the tide. As exposures of corruption in the executive branch grew more lurid, they agreed with him that the best strategy was to run for the presidency on a third-party ticket.

In 1923 La Follette began planning details so that the poor management of 1920 would not recur. Early in 1924 he mounted a nationwide campaign to collect signatures on petitions as a means of locating supporters. He sent his sons to find state and local leaders to manage his campaign. The first crisis came in March 1924 when he caught pneumonia. Belle and Robert Jr. begged him not to run, but, realizing how deeply he wanted the presidency, relented, still fearing that the strain would kill him. He went ahead.

By early 1924, the labor unions, Socialists, and farm groups turned to the Conference for Progressive Political Action as the focus for third-party activity. The startling success of the British Labour Party kindled hopes that American politics might also be realigned along ideological lines. From December 1922, when the CPPA celebrated its victories in the 1922 elections, until the national convention that would name a presidential candidate on July 4, 1924, the CPPA built a political movement from constituent interest groups. Every organization of workers, farmers, cooperative societies, and political parties would have three delegates to the convention; every state labor federation, railroad regulation group, or sympathetic committee of a state political party would have two; local labor and farm groups would have one. The delegates, in classic modernization style, would cast one vote for each 10,000 members they represented. But the convention would include significant representation from church groups that espoused the social gospel, from the National Association for the Advancement of Colored People, from campus political clubs, and from the League of Women Voters. Although the CPPA thus tried to forge a political movement incorporating the young, the women, the blacks, and the intellectuals under the leadership of farm and labor spokesmen, it kept the groups isolated as distinct blocs. The 1924 Progressive movement was a clear attempt to balance the spokesmen of separate and self-conscious groups whose only unity was their desire to oust conservative Republicans. La Follette alone had enough stature to give them any hope of victory.

Awaiting the CPPA convention, La Follette tackled one of the most difficult issues for a candidate appealing for radical support: communism. The issue had changed markedly for radicals from 1919 to 1924. In 1919 the Bolshevik Revolution implied a workers' democracy, and many workers agreed with La Follette that it provided a model worth considering and applying. In the early 1920s, however, as the Communists proved extremely effective politicians who could capture radical groups, resentment began to grow and bitter anti-Communist sentiment developed among radical groups like the Socialists, radical labor federations (like Chicago's), and labor unions. La Follette had been deeply disturbed during his 1923 visit to the Soviet Union by the suppression of free speech and free assembly and by the denial to the majority of access to political decisions. On May 26, 1924, he publicly refused to allow Communists to participate formally in his campaign. La Follette, and later the CPPA, took this stand not only to disarm conservative criticism, not only because they believed that Communists threatened civil liberties and majority rule, but also because, as a good politician, he profoundly respected and feared the Communists' ability to subvert his ambition. The Communists reciprocated by attacking La Follette more than the Republican and Democratic candidates.

La Follette announced his candidacy on July 3, 1924, the day before the CPPA would meet in Cleveland. He declared that "to break the combined power of the private monopoly system over the political and economic life of the American people is the one paramount issue." He emphasized the right of farmers and workers to resist monopoly by organizing. Not wanting to endanger progressive candidates in the two major parties, he opposed the creation of a third party that would nominate competing congressional and gubernatorial candidates.

The CPPA convention had a youthful, earnest air, perhaps because a majority of delegates were under 40. They improvised a fife and drum corps and choir to lead the entertainment. The more than 1000 delegates cheered the humanitarian poetry read by Edwin Markham, the invocation of Tom Johnson's memory by his old disciple Peter Witt, the conscience-stirring appeal from William Pickens of the NAACP, and the prediction of victory by New York Congressman Fiorello LaGuardia, who declared that "I speak for Avenue A and 116th Street, instead of Broad and Wall."

There was also a feeling of solidarity among the varied groups represented at the convention. The La Follette organization and railroad brotherhoods persuaded the Socialists to abandon plans for a formal third party until after the election. The convention enthusiastically "endorsed" La Follette, with seconding speeches from Morris Hillquit for the Socialists, Senator Lynn Frazier for the farmers, Harriet Stanton Blatch for the newly-enfranchised women, George Lefkowitz for the Farmer-Labor party, and William Pickens for the blacks. The campaign's executive committee also reflected the CPPA's desire to merge La Follette aides with representatives of the progressive blocs. Dominated by La Follette's political lieutenants and the railroad brotherhoods, the committee also included Mrs. Edward Costigan and Mrs. Glendower Evans to represent women voters, Frazier the farmers, and Hillquit the Socialists.

The first problem was to find a running mate. La Follette wanted a progressive Democrat, but his first choice, Justice

Louis Brandeis, turned him down. He then chose Montana Senator Burton K. Wheeler, an effective investigator of Harding's corruption who had refused to endorse the Democrats' nominee, John W. Davis, because he was too closely allied with Wall Street.

Soon after the convention, organizations pledged their support. Following Eugene Debs' advice, the Socialists formally endorsed La Follette at their July 7 convention. After failing to receive even polite consideration from the major parties, the American Federation of Labor very circumspectly supported La Follette and Wheeler. The railroad brotherhoods and other international unions soon enlisted. E. W. Scripps, La Follette's old friend, directed his chain of 25 newspapers to endorse La Follette, but this was La Follette's only significant support from newspapers.

Intellectuals and former insurgents, often reflecting the *Nation* and *New Republic,* championed the campaign. From New York in July came endorsements from W. E. B. DuBois, anthropologist Franz Boas, authors Theodore Dreiser and Thorstein Veblen, birth-control advocate Margaret Sanger, and Socialist clergyman Norman Thomas. When 1912 Progressives like James Garfield, Raymond Robins, Chester Rowell, and Gifford Pinchot invoked the memory of 1912 to support Coolidge, other 1912 Progressives — Harold Ickes, Gilson Gardner, Jane Addams, Francis Heney, Fremont Older, Amos Pinchot and George Record — rebuked them and supported La Follette. Ickes believed that his support for La Follette would lead him out of the GOP toward the Democrats who, in the future, would build on the base created by the 1924 La Follette movement. The *Cincinnati Enquirer* found 213 professors who supported La Follette and Wheeler. Offended by the Babbitt-like aspects of business civilization and believing that the power for change now resided in farmers and workers, these intellectuals agreed with Wilson's Assistant Labor Secretary Louis F. Post that La Follette's programs "tend to widen opportunities for productive enterprise and to promote fairness in the sharing of benefits."

The campaign took agonizing time to mobilize, suffering from lack of funds and the inexperience of its volunteers. Jealousy among John M. Nelson, the chairman, William T. Rawleigh, the treasurer, and Herman Ekern, an aide, slowed the Chicago headquarters. While Rawleigh felt "quite impatient" at "the apparent lack of business ability and capacity," Nelson complained that Rawleigh was so obsessed with official procedures "that weeks creep by before we get back letterheads and literature." Thus, by late August the campaign still lacked chairmen in eleven states. In late September the executive committee decided to place 50 speakers in the field if they did not cost more than $40,000. Another time the executive committee adjourned without a decision because it lacked $15,000 to organize the South. Local chairmen repeatedly complained about unclear directions.

La Follette's decision to lean heavily on trusted Wisconsin lieutenants had the same unhappy consequences as in the past. The most disastrous selection was that of his close friend Gilbert Roe to oversee the campaign in the Northeast. Roe's "utter lack of qualifications for practical political work," angered the man who should have managed the northeastern campaign, Fiorello LaGuardia, who "could have been of great service to us," according to Nelson. "Now we have drawn him in, put his career in jeopardy, and lost the benefit of his many points of contact and his large experience."

La Follette's campaign received its depth not from politicians, but from interest groups, particularly unions and especially railroad brotherhoods. When the deadline to file suddenly approached in Nevada, Nelson concluded that the only way to get signatures fast was to mobilize the brotherhoods there — and it worked. The brotherhoods decided on September 24 to cease all union work until after the campaign and to direct their more than 100 organizers to help local La Follette campaigns. Organized labor directed the Virginia campaign; the president of the Roanoke Central Trades Council organized the Roanoke La Follette campaign. Charles Kutz, a machinists' union official, sacrificed his union work in order to perform a more important job — director of the La Follette campaign in Pennsylvania.

But tensions within the labor movement retarded the campaign in other states. Although most unions and labor federations gave at least perfunctory endorsement to La Follette, others — including the Mine Workers, Pressmen, Carpenters, and the Central Trades and Labor Council of New York City, which switched its endorsement from La Follette to Davis five days before the election — endorsed his opponents. Differences between union leaders and Socialists hurt the campaign in Colorado, Kansas, Washington, Idaho, and Missouri.

La Follette, the major common element that had attracted the diverse elements, had to watch old antagonisms disrupt his campaign. In Buffalo cooperation was impossible by mid-October between the Labor-Socialist groups, which had the votes, and the middle-class La Follette-Wheeler Club, which had the respectability, according to a local organizer. From Wilkes-Barre came the complaint that the Pennsylvania campaign was "absolutely ignoring the progressives outside of the A.F. of L." Finally, many farmers were uneasy in a campaign that seemed completely dominated by unions and Socialists. "The southern and western farmer will not be the tail end of the labor kite," complained one, and most farm organizations did not even endorse La Follette.

The basic problem behind these tensions was modernization, which divided people according to their jobs. The *Louisville Post* explained that it would be "difficult, if not impossible, to hold together its many and conflicting interests and purposes." Higher farm prices meant lower real wages, and higher wages meant higher prices for goods farmers needed. Unions and farm organizations wanted security for their jobs and stable prices for their products. Further, interest group leaders (as opposed to rank-and-file workers and farmers) needed respectability when they dealt with businessmen and politicians, and they discovered hazards in a frontal attack on profit or the two major parties — hence the New York union reversal. They were torn between their own middle-class aspirations and their members' wishes in some cases. As workers and farmers accepted the permanence of their jobs, they also accepted a business-oriented attitude toward property and possessions. Finally, as farm and labor groups increasingly defined their goals in the narrowest needs of their members, they sought accommodation with senior congressmen whose committees prepared legislation in their areas. The farm bloc's approach had proved so successful in winning victories for farmers in the early twenties without raising larger issues or challenges to the two-party system that most farm groups shunned La Follette's broader third-party appeal.

In the Progressive platform of 1924, La Follette attempted to paper over differences between supporters and to adjust insurgent rhetoric to the new reality. The preamble declared that "the great issue" was the domination of private monopoly over consumers, but La Follette must have known this statement was only an echo of a dead movement because none of the specific planks promised anything to help consumers. The platform promised instead to end the "distress of American farmers" and to help workers organize to gain power. The tariff section appealed to farmers, not consumers. The platform also promoted "adequate laws to guarantee to farmers and industrial workers the right to organize and bargain collectively through representatives of their own choosing for the maintenance or improvement of their standards of life."

Even more menacing than the occupational differences that divided the Progressives' potential constituents were the bitter cultural conflicts, symbolized by prohibition and the rise of the Ku Klux Klan. Growing fastest in areas of rapid urbanization, the KKK had blossomed suddenly to preserve evangelical religion, enforce prohibition, and suppress blacks, Jews, and Catholics. The issue of the Klan ripped the 1924 Democratic convention to shreds. Condemning "any discrimination between races, classes and creeds," La Follette declared in a public letter to Robert P. Scripps: "I am unalterably opposed to the evident purposes of the secret organization known as the Ku Klux Klan." His forthright position won La Follette support from the NAACP as well as individual black leaders like DuBois, James Weldon Johnson, and Bishop John Hurst of the African Methodist Episcopal Church. Such endorsements only strengthened the conviction of the Klan's Imperial Wizard that La Follette was "the arch enemy of the nation."

Since the beginning of his political career La Follette had tried to subordinate such cultural conflicts to more important economic ones, but by 1924, as ethnic, religious, and racial tensions fragmented American society, La Follette found not only that he had earned the wrath of prohibitionist leaders as "the only wet candidate" but also that he could not even present his economic program without offending ethnic groups. His anti–Supreme Court plank, intended to rally organized labor, alarmed German Catholics and Lutherans who had found that the courts protected their parochial schools against Klan-dominated legislatures.

Along with these other worries, La Follette had financial problems. The Republican presidential campaign cost $4,270,469 and the Democratic campaign, $903,908; La Follette spent only $221,978. Labor unions did not support La Follette to the same extent that corporations supported the Republicans: 92 per cent of Republican funds came from corporations; unions probably contributed less than $50,000 to La Follette, with the AFL giving only $25,000. William T. Rawleigh paid one-eighth of the campaign's entire costs.

The La Follette campaign compensated for its lack of experience and money, however, with its zeal. Hiram Johnson observed that in California "all of the enthusiasm and the fervor in the campaign is in the La Follette camp." La Follette kicked off his campaign on Labor Day with a nationwide radio address appealing to farmers and workers to vote against monopoly-dominated government. Delayed by financial and organizational problems, he did not begin his speaking tour until October. He stumped in the Midwest and East, drawing the largest political audiences ever gathered at Rochester, Cincinnati, and Baltimore. But the climax came at his final speech in Cleveland, where 20,000 were "swept away in a frenzy almost religious."

The campaign began as a contest between Coolidge and La Follette. Many observers believed that the Wisconsin senator would carry enough states to force the election to the House, where Bryan might be elected. At the outset gamblers put the odds at 16 to 1 against a La Follette victory, but by mid-September these odds had shrunk to 6 to 1, rising slowly to 10 to 1 by late October and then rapidly to 35 to 1 on election day. Newspaper polls in September and October had revealed La Follette victories in Wisconsin, Minnesota, the Dakotas, Nebraska, Nevada, and Montana. He had finished second in the *Literary Digest's* poll of 2 million and the Hearst polls of over 600,000, both of which were concluded in mid-October.

The fundamental cause of La Follette's rapid decline was the inherent conservatism of modernization. Within a job-oriented politics, workers or farmers could choose only between getting more for their jobs (and supporting La Follette) or preserving the system of corporate control that produced the economic growth which provided their jobs and markets in the first place. Realizing this, businessmen and Republicans appealed to the conservative implications of the voters' job orientation through the press they largely controlled. They argued that conditions were improving for farmers and workers and that La Follette's election would cause a depression. The choice was "Coolidge or Chaos." La Follette's supporters repeatedly lamented that their largest single problem was to counteract Republican and manufacturer propaganda that a La Follette victory meant a depression. Workers' votes for Coolidge, wrote La Follette's Illinois chairman, were votes "of fear, fear of an industrial panic." John J. Hamilton reported from southern California that La Follette's supporters were afraid "to stand up against the jibe that they were a menace to prosperity."

Corporate leaders were frightened by the prospect of a class struggle, which they saw in La Follette's candidacy. The American Bankers Association told its state affiliates to mobilize all their members to defeat La Follette. Wholesalers and automobile dealers in North Dakota and California included in their contracts a provision that goods would not be delivered if La Follette won.

Although some farmers were intimidated by bankers who threatened to foreclose mortgages if La Follette won, the basic cause of his loss of support among farmers came from rising farm prices for the first time in several years. Hog and wheat prices rose more than 50 per cent from early July to October. In vain did Senator Henrik Shipstead charge that bankers and middlemen had carefully manipulated farm prices upward. Republicans further appealed to farmers by charging that huge urban unemployment would follow a La Follette victory, depriving farmers of their major market.

The success of the "Coolidge or Chaos" slogan showed that, when the test came in 1924, workers and farmers were unwilling to risk the "chaos" that a real threat to large-scale corporations might pose to the economic growth that provided their jobs and markets. It showed, too, that agreement on that assumption had replaced the prewar unity among consumers and taxpayers and the flirtation with a labor theory of value attacking middlemen and profiteers that had flickered briefly in 1919.

La Follette won 16.5 per cent of the votes, to 28.8 per cent for Davis and 54 per cent for Coolidge. He carried only Wisconsin (54 per cent) and placed second in eleven states north and west of Chicago: North Dakota (45 per cent), Minnesota (41), Montana (38), South Dakota and Idaho (37), Nevada and Washington (36), California (33), Wyoming (32), Iowa (28), and Oregon (25). Although his strong showing in these states superficially suggested rural support, he did better than his national average in 18 of the nation's 29 cities with populations over 250,000. He carried Milwaukee

(56 per cent) and finished second in counties containing San Francisco (45), Minneapolis (42), Cleveland (42), Pittsburgh (34), Toledo (31), Portland (28), Los Angeles (26), Rochester (22), Cincinnati (21) and Detroit (12).

La Follette's support came first and most obviously from previous Socialist voters, on whose ticket he ran in California, Missouri, New York, and Pennsylvania. Among the 217,000 Hearst readers who supported him, La Follette received 42 per cent of his vote from former Socialists. Listed in both Socialist and Progressive columns, he received more Socialist than Progressive votes in all ten of the New York City Assembly Districts that he carried but in only 6 of the 49 A.D.'s that he failed to carry.

Behind the Socialist support were the votes of many workers. Although La Follette carried half of the predominantly Jewish A.D.'s in New York City, his support among Jews was clearly divided by class. In the lower-class fourth and sixth A.D.'s on the Lower East Side La Follette got 42 per cent and 50 per cent, respectively, but he won only 10 per cent in the upper-middle class Jewish seventh and ninth A.D.'s in Central Park West. La Follette's 1924 vote in San Francisco correlated .97 with the vote on a 1916 antipicketing measure, as he clearly won the workers' votes and lost the support of those who believed workers had already gained too much. He carried Passaic County, New Jersey, where many workers had militant class feelings. His strong showing in Pittsburgh and western Pennsylvania resulted from the activities of that state's labor federation. And he won the support of railroad workers wherever they lived, from Nevada through small Missouri railroad towns to Cleveland.

But La Follette clearly did not win the support of a majority of the nation's workers, perhaps because they feared that they would lose their jobs, perhaps because ethnic commitments led them elsewhere. He received from a quarter to a third of the working-class Italian vote in New York, but only 15 per cent in the machine-oriented Irish fifteenth A.D. in

Brooklyn. Wheat farmers, who supported him in Minnesota and North Dakota, rejected him in Kansas.

Newspaper support was another crucial factor. He ran well in the few cities like Cleveland, Toledo, and Sacramento where major newspapers endorsed him.

As La Follette and his supporters asked why they had not done better, they returned to two causes: the campaign had tried to unite competing interest groups; and Coolidge was able to appeal to voters' job orientations better than La Follette. La Follette blamed the corporation-dominated press for the effectiveness of the Republican appeal. But many of his friends blamed the "treachery" of labor unions, particularly in the East. When his family attacked workers for deserting him, La Follette, ever the politician who understood popular sentiments, accused them of not understanding workers. "Those pay checks are all that stand between starvation for those workers and their families," he told them, and workers could not ignore the Republicans' job-oriented appeal. He also realized that rising farm prices caused his lack of farmer support.

Job-oriented politics also failed to resist corporate modernization because people's job interests were antagonistic. The hasty collapse of the CPPA and the withdrawal of farmer and worker groups immediately after the election confirmed this fact. La Follette explained to Rawleigh in 1925 that the CPPA had disintegrated because it had been "made up of various economic and political groups whose primary purposes were other than progressive political action." Hiram Johnson wrote Ickes that the "heterogeneous elements which ostensibly came together for La Follette could never be brought together under any one banner again."

The campaign took the toll his family had feared on La Follette's health. His heart deteriorated rapidly until he died of a heart attack on June 18, 1925, four days after his seventieth birthday. The next day, the casket was loaded aboard the private car that had carried him on the campaign, for his last journey from Washington to Madison. In rail centers, workers doffed their caps to salute him as the car passed by. Knots of people waved to the train as it moved through southern Wisconsin. Thousands awaited its arrival in Madison. During the eight hours the casket was available for public viewing in Madison, some 50,000 people passed by the bier, bringing wild flowers and wreaths. And then he was buried in Madison, where his career had begun.

The national attention to his death and funeral was greater, perhaps, than that given fallen presidents. David K. Niles of Boston wrote Belle for millions: "He inspired me as no other man ever did. In my opinion he was our greatest American." Burton Wheeler ranked La Follette with Jefferson and Lincoln as the three greatest Americans: Jefferson, because he had written the Declaration of Independence; Lincoln, because he had emancipated the slaves; and La Follette, because he was the foremost champion of industrial emancipation. The "dear old rotten Senate," as La Follette had called it early in his career, voted two generations later that he had been one of its five greatest members, along with Clay, Calhoun, Webster, and Robert A. Taft.

But, in the deepest sense, La Follette's career and his death in 1925 showed the collapse of two possible bases for resistance to large-scale industrial capitalism: the consumer-taxpayer-citizen base that had catapulted him to fame in the first decade of the twentieth century as part of insurgency, and the farmer-worker alliance after the war that had supported his presidential campaign. As the major institutions of American life — the corporations, the press, the schools, the unions, and the farm groups — one by one came to accept modernization based on corporate-sponsored economic growth, La Follette sounded increasingly anachronistic to his supporters as he continued to insist that the only basic solution was to attack concentrated wealth and power.

La Follette's career had truly encompassed the rise and fall of insurgency. After his death a few leaders like Huey Long in the 1930s or Ralph Nader in the 1960s and 1970s would echo La Follette's attacks on large corporate power, but even they lacked the old insurgent trust in direct popular rule. And, as they struggled against modernizing groups and institutions, they had greater cause than most to understand the exhaustion of the anticorporate tradition that La Follette had personified. The qualities that impressed most mourners in 1925 were his courage, bravery, and fearlessness, for they knew that he had failed to establish the society he envisioned. He was remembered as Fighting Bob.

A Note on the Sources

The Robert M. La Follette, Sr. Papers formed the basic source for this book. The papers for his state career (1879–1905) are housed at the State Historical Society of Wisconsin, and those for his senatorial activities (1906–1925) are at the Library of Congress. The La Follette family collection at the Library of Congress also includes the papers of Belle, Fola, and Robert M. La Follette, Jr. The Philip F. La Follette Papers are at the State Historical Society of Wisconsin. *La Follette's Weekly Magazine* (1909–1914) and *La Follette's Magazine* (a monthly, 1914–1925) contained La Follette's editorials (often condensed from Senate speeches), revealed his understanding of the progressive movement through his choice of articles, and described the family's activities. The (Madison) *University Press,* which La Follette edited from 1876 to 1879 (housed at Memorial Library, University of Wisconsin), reveals his perspective on his college education. The (Madison) *Old Dane* (1897–1898) and *The State* (1898–1900), and the (Milwaukee) *Free Press* (1901–1905) were the semi-official newspapers for his insurgent Republican faction in Wisconsin. The *Congressional Record* was essential for his House (1885–1891) and Senate (1906–1925) careers, and the *Journals* of the Wisconsin Assembly and Senate (1901–1905) contained his gubernatorial messages and vetoes.

Since insurgents like La Follette were not introspective, it was essential to consult the private collections of his associates. The Papers of George W. Norris, Gifford Pinchot, Albert J. Beveridge, and Ray Stannard Baker at the Library of Congress contained revealing comments about La Follette, but the papers of the California progressives were the most helpful for understanding La Follette's effect on progressivism as a national movement. The Papers of Hiram

Johnson and Chester H. Rowell were the largest and most political, but the Papers of John Works and the slim Francis J. Heney collection (all at the Bancroft Library, University of California at Berkeley) contained the most frequent ideological reflections. The papers of the National Progressive Republican League, the Conference for Progressive Political Action, and the La Follette-Wheeler Campaign Committee (all at the Library of Congress) were important for La Follette's 1912 and 1924 presidential campaigns. For La Follette's Wisconsin career the most useful collections were those of Elisha W. Keyes, Willet S. Main, Albert R. Hall, Nils P. Haugen, Charles R. Van Hise, and Richard T. Ely, all at the State Historical Society of Wisconsin.

This book has relied on dozens of journalistic accounts for its interpretation of La Follette's significance to movements and events. The basic newspaper sources were the *Milwaukee Sentinel* before 1901, and the *Washington Post, Chicago Tribune,* and *New York Times* for his senatorial career.

The La Follette family published an unusually large number of books to describe and justify La Follette's activities. The natural places to begin are *La Follette's Autobiography: A Personal Narrative of Political Experiences* (1911, 1913), a campaign tract for his 1912 presidential campaign, and Belle Case and Fola La Follette, *Robert M. La Follette* (2 vols., 1953). The most convenient introduction to La Follette's ideas is Ellen Torelle, ed., *The Political Philosophy of Robert M. La Follette* (1920).

La Follette's career in Wisconsin has received far greater attention from scholars than his senatorial activities, largely because the collection of his papers at the Library of Congress has only opened recently to scholars. Elaboration and documentation for chapters 1 and 2 of this book can be found in David P. Thelen, *The Early Life of Robert M. La Follette, 1855–1884* (1966) and *The New Citizenship: Origins of Progressivism in Wisconsin, 1885–1900* (1972). La Follette's Wisconsin activities have been described in Robert S. Maxwell, *La Follette and the Rise of the Progressives in Wisconsin* (1956); Herbert F. Margulies, *The Decline of the Progressive Movement in Wisconsin, 1890–1928* (1968); Allen F. Lovejoy, *La Follette and the Establishment of the Direct Primary in Wisconsin* (1941); Stanley P. Caine, *The Myth of a Progressive Reform: Railroad Regulation in Wisconsin, 1903–1910* (1970) — a splendid case study;

Albert O. Barton, *La Follette's Winning of Wisconsin, 1894–1904* (1922) ; Carroll Pollack Lahman, "Robert Marion La Follette as a Public Speaker and Political Leader, 1855–1905" (unpublished Ph.D. dissertation, University of Wisconsin, 1939) ; Wallace S. Sayre, "Robert M. La Follette: A Study in Political Methods" (unpublished Ph.D. dissertation, New York University, 1930) ; Robert C. Twombly, "The Reformer as Politician: Robert M. La Follette in the Election of 1900" (unpublished M.A. thesis, University of Wisconsin, 1966) ; Kenneth C. Acrea, Jr., "Wisconsin Progressivism: Legislative Response to Social Change, 1891 to 1909" (unpublished Ph.D. dissertation, University of Wisconsin, 1968) ; Roger E. Wyman, "Voting Behavior in the Progressive Era: Wisconsin as a Case Study" (unpublished Ph.D. dissertation, University of Wisconsin, 1970) and "Middle Class Voters and Progressive Reform: The Conflict of Class and Culture," *American Political Science Review*, 68 (June 1974), 488–504. The best case study of the meaning of insurgent rhetoric to grassroots Wisconsin is easily Paul H. Hass, "The Suppression of John F. Deitz: An Episode of the Progressive Era in Wisconsin," *Wisconsin Magazine of History*, 57 (Summer 1974) .

La Follette's national career is the focus for Eugene A. Manning, "Old Bob La Follette: Champion of the People" (unpublished Ph.D. dissertation, University of Wisconsin, 1966); Kenneth C. MacKay, *The Progressive Movement of 1924* (1947) ; Padraic Colum Kennedy, "La Follette's Foreign Policy: From Imperialism to Anti-Imperialism," *Wisconsin Magazine of History*, 46 (Summer 1963) .

The writings of La Follette's contemporaries defined the context of his activities. Benjamin Parke DeWitt, *The Progressive Movement* (1915) remains the best contemporary description. Contours of insurgency are revealed in J. Allen Smith, *The Spirit of American Government* (1907) ; David Graham Phillips, *The Treason of the Senate* (1906) ; Edward A. Ross, *Sin and Society* (1907) ; and Ben B. Lindsey and Harvey J. O'Higgins, *The Beast* (1910) . Modernization can be traced through John R. Commons, *Myself* (1934) ; Charles McCarthy, *The Wisconsin Idea* (1912) ; and Herbert Croly, *The Promise of American Life* (1909) . La Follette liked and respected Lincoln Steffens, along with Commons and Louis Brandeis, most among intellectuals, and Steffens has left a classic appraisal in his *Autobiography* (1931) and his portrait of five insurgents, *Upbuilders* (1909) .

Several studies of other insurgent Republican senators provided valuable perspective: Kenneth W. Hechler, *Insurgency: Personalities and Politics of the Taft Era* (1940); James Holt, *Congressional Insurgents and the Party System, 1909–1916* (1967); Claude G. Bowers, *Beveridge and the Progressive Era* (1932); John Braeman, *Albert J. Beveridge, American Nationalist* (1971); Richard Lowitt, *George W. Norris* (2 vols., 1963, 1971); Leroy Ashby, *The Spearless Leader: Senator Borah and the Progressive Movement in the 1920's* (1972). Books on the two presidents who most deeply angered La Follette offered essential background information: Henry F. Pringle, *Theodore Roosevelt* (1931); John M. Blum, *The Republican Roosevelt* (1954); George E. Mowry, *Theodore Roosevelt and the Progressive Movement* (1946); William H. Harbaugh, *The Life and Times of Theodore Roosevelt* (1963 ed.); Arthur S. Link, *Wilson* (5 vols., 1947–1966).

Some studies of progressivism in the cities and states were particularly helpful: George E. Mowry, *The California Progressives* (1951); Michael P. Rogin and John L. Shover, *Political Change in California* (1970); Walton Bean, *Boss Ruef's San Francisco* (1952); Carl H. Chrislock, *The Progressive Era in Minnesota* (1971); Hoyt Landon Warner, *Progressivism in Ohio, 1897–1917* (1964); Ransom E. Noble, *New Jersey Progressivism Before Wilson* (1946); Melvin G. Holli, *Reform in Detroit: Hazen S. Pingree and Urban Politics* (1969); J. Joseph Huthmacher, "Charles Evans Hughes and Charles Francis Murphy: The Metamorphosis of Progressivism," *New York History*, 46 (January 1965), 25–40; Arthur Mann, *LaGuardia* (2 vols., 1959, 1965); Robert Sherman La Forte, *Leaders of Reform: Progressive Republicans in Kansas, 1900–1916* (1974); John D. Buenker, *Urban Liberalism and Progressive Reform* (1973).

Although space limitations prevent acknowledgement of all the monographs that have enriched this book, a few major interpretations proved particularly stimulating. Richard Hofstadter, *The Age of Reform from Bryan to FDR* (1955) remains a challenging book, and its discussion of consumer consciousness has received little of the attention it merits. Samuel P. Hays, *The Response to Industrialism* (1957) and Robert H. Wiebe, *The Search for Order* (1967) have so effectively charted the process described in this book as modernization that their framework has shaped the bulk of subsequent studies of this period. Gabriel Kolko's *The Triumph of Conservatism: A Rein-*

terpretation of American History, 1900–1916 (1963) and *Railroads and Regulation, 1877–1916* (1965) describe how large corporations came to dominate the process of modernization, although Kolko locates the "triumph" considerably earlier than this book. Insurgent progressivism received its vitality from the merger in consumer and taxpayer consciousness of two social and political cultures that had clashed repeatedly in nineteenth-century America. James Willard Hurst, *Law and the Conditions of Freedom in the Nineteenth Century United States* (1956) brilliantly explores values that made a market economy so attractive at first; and Michael J. Cassity's case study of Sedalia, Missouri, "Defending a Way of Life" (unpublished Ph.D. dissertation, University of Missouri, 1973) penetratingly reveals patterns of resistance to market values.

Index